Pirating
Plants

Propagation for the amateur gardener

Pirating Plants

by Peter Tobey

with illustrations by the author

Tobey Publishing Co., Inc.

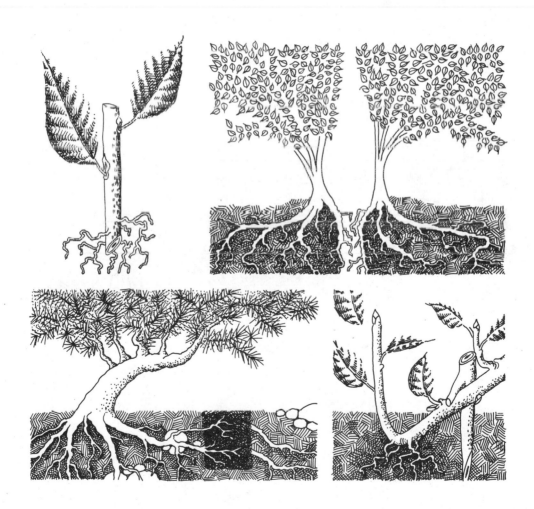

Contents

Chapter 1

I'm not sure that this book does what it is supposed to do. I'm not certain that if you read it you will get everything out of it that I would like you to. But I guess that writers never really know if they are getting their points across. Wondering about it is a gnawing kind of anxiety that I'm not used to and don't like. I suppose that if lots of people buy a book, you can assume that the few who first read it liked it and suggested that their friends read it too. But, you can never be sure if that's what's happening. The people who read your book aren't around to tell you what they think of it. In fact, they may be liking or disliking the thing for all the wrong reasons. That's bewildering. It means, in effect, that I don't really know what's in this book even though I've been paying close attention to it for some time now. I'm not sure I've managed what I was attempting here and I'm feeling a little weird about it.

If I knew more people who made their livings with words, I would probably feel better about the whole thing. The one or two I know have a tendency to call each other on the phone all the time and ask how it's going. I do that too. We are looking, I think, for some reassurance that it's going lousy for everybody and that we are not alone in our starings at a blank piece of paper propped in a typewriter. More to the point, perhaps, is the odd feeling that, when you're done, no one is going to laugh at your jokes, be moved by your sincerities or be concerned at all with your subject matter. This probably explains the writer's love of reading his own words aloud. When you read what you've written to people, you can see if they like it by such tip-offs as smiling, laughing, clapping their hands, falling on the floor and asking questions. Having read this book to a couple of friends, I've noticed that it's generally me who ends up clapping my hands and laughing. I really like this book. I liked writing it. I said just what I wanted to, just the way I wanted to. And it felt good. But now that I've had all that fun, I wonder if anybody will understand, enjoy or even care about the thing. I've spent lots of time writing words and drawing pictures and I'm still not certain you will get the drift of what I think about pirating plants. So, in case I blew it in the rest of the book, I'm going to tell you straight out what I think is important here.

When other writers decide that they don't feel confident about the body of their books, they add a series of clues at the beginning called an introduction. But I've noticed, in watching myself read, that I never read the introductions to books that are supposed to tell me how to do something. I am not interested in hearing some guy tell me what he feels about the doing. I just want to know how to do it. Listening to the quasi-philosophical or psychological ramblings surrounding a practical problem that requires concrete answers seems to me to be a waste of time. So I skip the introductions. And pirating plants, like cooking or bicycling, is a practical problem that requires answers.

But there's a point about plants and gardening that I want to make here, just in case I haven't made it well enough elsewhere. And I wanted you to read it, so I called this Chapter 1 instead of the Introduction. My apologies.

I think that the most important thing you can get out of my book is a feeling for the good times, tilting laughter and self-satisfied, blithering pleasure that I get out of plant propagation. I love it. And I think that if you go at it properly, the spirit of your doing it will affect your skills or, at least, your appraisal of those skills. I've tried to give this book that feeling but it may not have worked. So, here, in the introduction, is my last chance to try.

'Pirating,' as you've probably figured out by now, is code for propagating. Propagating means reproducing, making new. Pirating, then, means reproducing plants with swashbuckling good humor and a sense of thievery about you. The two words mean pretty much the same thing and I use them interchangeably throughout this book and with little attention to my choice. But there is that difference of attitude that I've tried to indicate indirectly as I went along.

Propagating connotes to me the efficient, practiced and purposeful growing of plants. Commercial nurseries 'propagate.' Pirating is a much messier, less effective, extremely inefficient madness that possesses a person when he discovers that he loves plants, is awed by their ability to reproduce and either can't afford or isn't inclined to simply buy them full grown from a nursery. I confess here and now that I have not yet had the opportunity to find out if I would buy them already mature if I could. I can't afford it. All I know is that even though I'm forced to search for free plants, I find I don't mind at all. If he were here, Milton would point out that I have taken advantage of and pleasure from my fallen position. *Felix culpa* was his expression. But, I think I just like playing in the garden, messing with the dirt and would have found a way to do it even if I had all the money in the world.

My point is that the pirating of plants is nifty. You gather bits and pieces of plants without harming them and turn those pieces into new plants. There's a serendipitous quality to it. Free stuff that grows. And I want everybody to know how great it is so that they can enjoy it themselves. Follow the remarkable, prolific, pleasant spirit of the enterprise to its hilt. Don't worry overmuch about it. Try hard, pay attention and enjoy your failures as well as your successes. A successfully rooted cutting is no more or less important than the childish fun of feeling dirt under your fingernails. The percentage of plants successfully pirated in any one batch of attempts is almost irrelevant in light of the clumsy fun of trying. The sophistication of your equipment, the honing of your skills, the breadth of your knowledge and all that sort of 'how-to' stuff isn't so important as the extent to which you can enjoy escaping into the world of wee and struggling plants that are making such a wonderful effort to be.

Expeditions

There's something fantastical about the spirit of an expedition. Something unreal that bothers people. For most of us, it's almost impossible to imagine going on one and the images that the word conjures serve to discourage even trying. The very idea sounds a little half-witted. Children go on expeditions, hunting for shells and pebbles on the beach. Bums make a life's work of it simply because they have no where to stay. And then there are those maniacs, doomed to frostbite and worse, who go to the Poles and squint at the snow. Expeditions seem either silly or tend to require too much equipment and hardship to make any sense.

When you add to the foolishness of expeditions the idea of looking for free stuff while wandering around, you've got a looney-tune concept on your hands. And any normal person's reaction to it is aggravated further by the long-ingrained resolve that you won't find a damn thing even if you look for it. Nothing's free, Bah Humbug, and the only people who think so are panhandlers and welfare chisellers. The age of the pioneer is over. You can't homestead anymore. Finding and collecting is neither a successful nor healthy way to acquire things. It's not normal, it's un-American and you shouldn't do it.

Well, to hell with that.

It may be true, but I'm not going to believe it. I've decided very consciously to nurture whatever expeditionary, pooh-bear lunacy I've got left. In spite of superior arguments to the contrary, I'm not going to give up my faith in the possibility of finding things that are free but valuable. Of course, I'm an adult of sorts and reasonably sane, so I can't maintain too many illusions too long if they are frequently challenged by very real failure. But, rather than give up altogether, I amend my techniques and objectives to the point where they work and still more or less fit into my pipe dreams.

That's how I became involved in pirating plants. Not by way of an original immersion in horticulture. Such people become involved in propagation. I came to my madness through the combined influence of expeditionary interest, plant love and strong tendencies toward both compassion and greed.

Let me explain.

I love plants. I love having them around. I love taking care of them. I love watching them grow up. But I *really* get a kick out of the challenge of finding free but nevertheless remarkable plants in the most unsuspected places. I like exchanging them with friends and I like walking through the woods with a shovel, some polyethylene and a silly grin.

Before anyone begins to think nasty thoughts about my ravishing national parks of vulnerable, nearly extinct varieties of shrubbery, let me say that I don't: I don't. What I do is grope around anyone's property who will allow it. Here's where the compassion comes in. Any 3/4 acre lot that has been planted for ten or fifteen years, and not exactly manicured during that time, almost always will contain a variety of struggling plants that are better off moved. So, after having secured permission, I move them.

I find straggly, leggy shrubs, doomed volunteer seedlings dying in the shade and a wealth of seeds, cuttings, etc., even in the best kept of properties. I save this abused and misused treasure from being ignored. I take care of it. I help it grow. See the compassion.

Now for the greed. Without paying anything, I end up with absurdly-beautiful specimens. And I have a lot of fun doing it.

Perhaps the most challenging form of pirating plants is an attempted transplanting. There are, of course, methods of propagating cuttings and roots and other bits and pieces of a plant when the whole of it can't be taken. But on those occasions when I am allowed to make off with an entire tree or shrub, I sometimes stumble upon the luck to discover and transport a natural dwarf or twisted seedling. And after pruning and care, I often end up with a beautiful thing that never would have been beautiful if left where it was.

Some transplantings are very easy. Volunteer seedlings can hardly be destroyed if dug at the right time and with even the slightest amount of care. Other finds are more difficult however.

These are wild sparkleberry, one of which has survived the erosion that has exposed its roots. It's twisted and marred wild specimens like these, seemingly staggering down hill, that make pirating plants such a peculiar pleasure.

Natural dwarfs, large shrubs or reasonably-sized trees can be tricky to dig. Not, certainly, difficult to get out of the ground, but difficult to keep alive afterwards.

Before getting too involved in this how-to discussion of shrub and tree removal, I should mention a few basics on plant life that relate to transplanting.

Plants live and grow by receiving a steady supply of water, air, soil nutrients and sunlight. They combine these resources and both maintain and add to their foliage and roots. If there proves to be a

19

deficiency of any of these resources a plant must reduce its activity and growth to fit the scope of its inputs. Plants can't work with what they don't have and so cut back on their entire operations to suit their environments.

Thus, a tree that has difficulty getting water will be small and have few leaves. It may have all the sun that it can use, or more than it needs, but if the water isn't there the plant won't grow. This interdependent nature of raw materials keeps plants balanced in their growth. Their above and below-ground activity fits their environment.

But there is an even more remarkable interrelation at work too. This one balances not only the entire plant's growth to its environment but also the parts of a plant one to the other. That is, the leaves and roots grow together, affected one by the other. Roots and leaves are interdependent since one part of a plant grows by using the products of the entire plant's production. So, you can grow more leaves only if you have a root system big enough to support it. And you can grow more roots only if the leaves are feeding enough energy to them. Not only that, but if one part gets ahead of another, there will be a sort of hyper-supply of energy to the laggard part until it grows and so catches up. This kind of interrelation means that one part of a plant will grow as fast as its other parts force it to. Assuming a good supply of raw materials.

Now, wait a minute. What's controlling plant growth here? I just said that a plant grows as fast as its most deficient source will allow. Then I said that a plant tends to grow as fast as its most vigorous part. One might sense a contradiction there. But, in fact, this very forcing of other parts to thrive is the basis for all propagation by asexual means. Cuttings without roots force roots to grow. Roots without stems and leaves form them. All this balancing out, this following of the most successful level of growth is, as I said before, dependent on a ready supply of raw materials.

Clearly, there's a rather tricky balance involved here. Plants stay in almost perfect balance all the time, having neither more nor less above-ground growth than the roots can support. It's for this reason that a container plant usually grows if transplanted into a larger pot. Roots grow to fill the pot and so supply the top growth with the good things it needs to grow as well.

Everybody seems to know that healthy and growing roots make for larger plants. What people don't think about is that the energy from top growth is that which forces roots to develop. If, for one reason or another, the top of a plant outgrows its root system, energy is diverted to developing more roots to support the top. And those roots grow and thrive if the soil around them is suitable. And now that I've finally worked my way around to it and found a decent way of expressing the phenomenon, it's easy to understand.

The basic challenge in transplanting trees and shrubs is in preserving as much of the plant's root system as possible. If you hack up the roots in getting the top of the plant home, that cherished top is doomed. But it is often difficult to get a sizable portion of the roots when you dig up a plant.

An example or two may help illustrate. I've a friend with a friend whose uncle owns some property that used to be an apple orchard. (I compulsively trace such connections for the sake of such finds.) Anyway, one weekend I journeyed to this barren but not moribund orchard and found rows of trees gone bad. Not dead, but little more than trunks with bits of languishing and unproductive growth. One of them had somehow produced an apple that by squirrel or other carrier had found its way into a stone wall that edged the property. The sapling that had grown there was thin and twisted. Its roots wound through the wall and its trunk curved gently around a bolder.

The root systems of such trees are strung out all over the place. In order to survive, they have searched for the moisture and nutrients they need. Digging them is difficult because you can't get enough soil and root to support the tree. Adding to the problems, these natural dwarfs are often old and slow growing. They lack the vigor to recover from the setback of digging. They require great care, greater patience and still almost never survive if transplanted immediately.

You may run into the same sort of problem with a large, healthy bush. To support its top growth, it produces a large and spreading root system. In order to preserve the thing, you have to bring as much of that system along with you as you can when you leave.

With almost any large plant and certainly with any one that has a widely spread or sparse root network, some form of planning and preparation is necessary. The amount of preparation is controlled by the amount of top growth you wish to preserve. A small seedling needs almost no special efforts. A shrub that you intend to cut back sharply needs little or none. (Pruning back the top reduces the demands on the root system and so makes it possible for a reduced number of roots to support the plant. But more on that later.) But a tree or bush that is six-feet tall and that you would like to keep almost that height, or one that has a hundred feet of rambling, runaway roots, needs some work ahead of time. And it's here that we separate those who are simply enchanted by my sterling prose from those who want to pirate plants on a truly grand scale. Those of you who are interested in easy plant propagation won't be interested in transplanting difficult shrubs and trees. There's nothing easy about it. Preparing a large plant or naturally dwarfed tree for transplanting can take a couple of years. In some cases only one full season, but in others, two. And that's a lot of work for your bush.

(I told you in the beginning you had to be a little daft to go in for all of this. For those of you who aren't interested in this sort of long-term investment, bear with me. I come up with some great short cuts later on.)

Most dead transplantings are the result of a failure to gather enough root with the foliage. The solution is obvious: force the plant to grow all or most of its roots in one place. It's this idea of control that has led to the extensive use of containers in modern nurseries. Shrubs and trees grown in buckets can be moved during any season and transplanted with little worry because all of the root system necessary for the support of the plant is moved with it. The roots of plants growing in the ground, however, grow every which way. And long. But you can encourage them to concentrate their growth in a small area so that later you can dig it all up.

In order to force root growth in a confined area in a plant that has grown freely for a long time, you have to cut back those roots that are spreading. This can be done in a number of ways, with varying degrees of success. However, all of the following steps should be taken when the plant is dormant. In the case of deciduous trees, the timing is clear—when the leaves fall. Evergreens, however, are never so completely dormant and tend also to grow more slowly. But, balancing this lethargy is their reduced demands on a root system in the first place. Since evergreens don't have to produce huge quantities of foliage every year, they can survive more easily on fewer roots.

All of which boils down to, basically, the need to root prune in the very late fall or winter. A radical reduction in the supply from the roots won't hurt the tree much at that time, since it is dormant and making reduced demands.

The simplest method of root pruning is to sharpen a flat-bladed shovel and make alternate cuts into the soil around the tree. This should be done at about the same distance from the plant as you intend later to ball it. Most gardeners will tell you that you should cut into the ground about half way between the trunk and the spread of the leaves. Either way, you should end up cutting roots to about a 12 to 18 inch length.

The severed outside roots die. The shortened inside roots are forced to grow because of the imbalance between root system and foliage. All the new growth (or most of it) is inside the shovel cuts and so a greater proportion of root is removed a year later when the tree is transplanted.

If the tree is very large, you can wait a year and then make shovel insertions, filling in the gaps you left before.

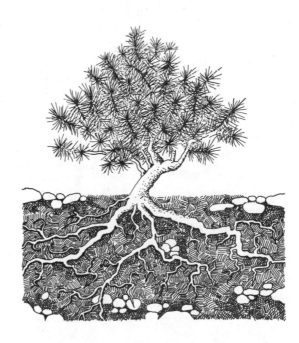

This method of root pruning keeps some roots intact so that the shock to the plant won't be too severe. But, if you're impatient or can water the pruned tree if it gets dry during the year it takes to recover, you can prune all the way around the roots in the first year and have done with it, one way or another.

Another method of root pruning, and one that I like better for such problems as my apple tree in the wall (remember my apple tree in the wall?), is to dig a trench around the trunk about 8 inches away from it and about 6 inches wide. Go as deep as you have to or can manage. Not surprisingly, as you dig you'll run into several roots. Hopefully, you'll run into lots of them. Cut 'em. If you feel patient or hope especially for the survival of your find, you can also paint the cut ends of the roots with rooting hormone. After having circled (or

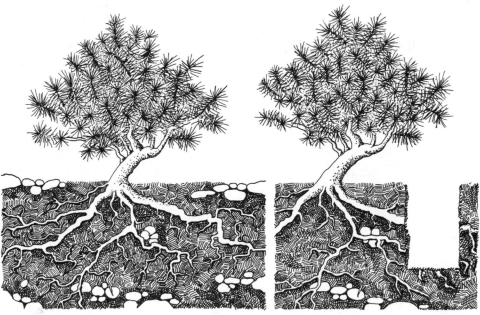

A wild, small pine with a widely spreading root structure that has been chosen for transplanting. If it were simply dug, even with a relatively large root ball, it would probably die.

So a trench is dug around the tree, cutting through several roots. The ends of these roots are coated with rooting hormone.

24

half-circled, as in the shovel method above) the tree, fill the trench with your finest potting soil mixture carefully prepared to your specimen's taste. This wonderful soil encourages new roots to form so the ball is compact and healthy when you dig it up at the end of its growing season.

When to Expedition

Root pruning is carried on during dormancy so that in the spring, when the plant begins to grow again, its energies are directed toward producing new roots. Top growth is held to a minimum and all the plant's energies go underground.

Transplanting should occur at the same time, in the very late winter or very early spring. Many tomes written on the subject

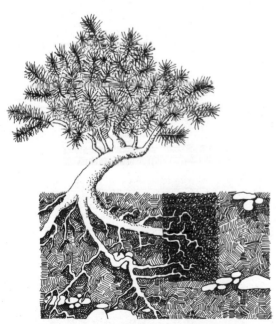

The trench is filled with rich soil. After a year roots will have grown closer to the tree on the main roots that remained and the soil in the trench should be loaded with them. This more compact root structure makes for easier transplanting.

Just for fun I pruned this one into a bonsai.

suggest that you dig *just before* the buds of new growth begin to swell. That sort of advice is annoying. It's rather like being asked to get off a bus one stop before a friend when you don't know where he's getting off. My advice is simpler. Think, throughout the cold months of winter, of the pleasures of spring. Consider often the long days of new green that are approaching. Dream a lot about your garden. Then wait. The very moment you can stand it no longer and feel absolutely compelled to walk around in the world, even though your head knows it's not quite yet spring, then you'll know that your bones are right and it's time to dig.

The only other time that transplanting is reasonably safe is in the early fall. By then, new growth has become almost as dark as the old. At this time, there is still enough season left for the roots to grow and reestablish themselves before winter. But late summer and fall transplanting must be accompanied by considerable top pruning. Which, by the way, comes next.

Pruning

Regardless of any steps that you've taken before actually digging up the plant, you're bound to disrupt it when you do. Even if the roots are compact and in the right place, you'll jar them, causing some to separate from the soil. Being transplanted is a difficult thing for a sizable plant. No matter what, its root system is going to be diminished.

To prevent this smaller and less effective root system from trying to keep all of the original top growth alive, thereby failing to keep any of it alive, you should prune before digging. Don't simply cut back, however. Consider the thing carefully, studying and enjoying its strengths and weaknesses. Find those branches that are most attractive, those that you later want to encourage and those that you want to remove regardless. Thin the plant, cutting some branches back all the way to the trunk. Trim it and get it reduced to about 1/2 or 2/3 of its original size. Be ruthless. Be careful. You can't put anything back.

If, for one reason or another, the ultimate success of transplanting seems doubtful to you, you might try an antidesiccant. This is a latex-based plastic spray used by nurserymen on difficult transplantings. It coats the leaves of the plant to reduce evaporation after the transplanting, thereby reducing the demands made of the

This is a simple illustration of how you can prune a shrub about to be transplanted without making it look as though it has simply been sheared.

roots. Antidessicants let light and air pass through them but hold water.

A similar technique is to treat your transplanted find much like a seedling or cutting. You can put it in a cold frame or, lacking one, cover it with polyethylene plastic for the first month or so of its life in a new home. Polyethylene may sound forbidding, but it's nothing more than the stuff sandwich bags are made of. The plastic, like the latex film, allows air and sun to pass but holds water in a confined environment around the leaves.

Regardless of whether you use latex and plastic bags, you should spray the foliage of the plant with water. If you can, periodically repeat the spraying while you dig. It's a logical excuse to stop working for a while.

Digging

Most beginning or unschooled transplant artists put shovel to ground and lift as large a hunk of dirt out around the roots as they can carry. Wrong. Wrong. Wrong. Doing so cuts many roots that extend beyond the ball. The idea here should be to take as much soil as you can lift but also preserve as much root as possible that extends beyond the ball.

Unless you've never really recovered from the sandbox syndrome of tirelessly playing in the dirt, you probably won't enjoy digging large plants. But then, you probably won't like gardening either. What it takes is a trowel, not a shovel, and a considerable amount of patience.

Start digging about three feet away from the base of the trunk. If the prize is quite small, start a little closer. Dig a trench much like

27

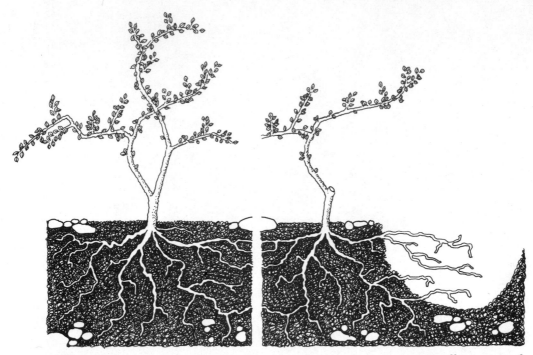

A Cotoneaster being transplanted. Note the grotesque but encouraging illustration of salvaged roots that are outside the root ball. Also, the plant has been pruned before digging.

the one described above but make it continually wider as you go. Basically, you're digging your way toward the root ball rather than trying to lift it out. The advantage of this technique is that, as you go, you *don't* cut the roots. Rather, brush the soil off of them and leave them bare but intact. Be especially careful not to damage the smallest of the roots, the tiny whitish hairs. It's these that do the actual drinking, the bigger ones just transport what they've guzzled. If the digging takes awhile, and it does, spray these fine root hairs periodically. If they dry out, they become very brittle and are likely to break.

Work your way into the root ball until it is anywhere from 1 to 2 feet in diameter, again, depending on the size of the plant. As you go deeper, you'll probably find fewer and fewer roots spreading from the basic soil ball you intend to lift. This is because most roots stay on the surface in the top soil and moisture. However, you'll come upon the tap root at the very bottom. It is a large, strong root going straight down. Many people believe it is the 'heart' of the root system and feel that shortening it radically kills the plant. However, tap roots are, with the exception of pines, nothing but large roots intended to hold the plant up in the wind. They also gather moisture and nutrients like other roots, but are no more important than the others. The idea in cutting the tap root is to take as much of it as you can. But don't be afraid of it. If the tap root seems to be an enormous part of the root system, then cut it very long and try winding it around the root ball.

Burlap

Once the root ball is actually dug, you should spray it again with water. Then wrap the whole ball in water-soaked burlap and tie it up. Apply a layer of plastic around the burlap. And then tie that up.

Actually lifting the root ball from its hole and tying it is a crucial time in the plant's life. Consider it exactly as it is, a kind of amputation. The plant is now completely severed from almost all of the environment that it has ever known. The only home it's taking with it is in the ball. Be careful then not to crack or shake that familiar remnant. If you do, you'll dislodge what few roots are still firmly attached and surrounded by soil. Be very gentle.

In wrapping the burlap, don't be afraid to make it tight. Air pockets can dry the roots and a sloppy tying job allows the soil ball to disintegrate. If, after the thing is wrapped, you've got a gap between the burlap and the soil, pour some dirt in. Then water that dirt thoroughly.

I refuse to belabor the obvious care you should give your treasure en route from the digs to your home. Say nice things to it, spray its foliage if it seems to be drying out and avoid large bumps in the road.

Planting

Plant quickly. If you're really on the ball, you'll have already dug a large hole for the transplant. Make that hole at least 8 inches deeper than the root ball requires and a full 6 inches wider. Space the dangling roots that are (still moist) outside the ball and fill in around them with porous soil. Use dry soil and water it later.

Planting is one of those things that is best explained in pictures, so one is included here. However, note that if you have cut the tap root radically and the tree is tall, you should tie it so that it won't blow over.

Care and Feeding

Soak the root ball, surrounding soil and leaves. You might even build a dam of sorts around the root area to hold additional water. But be sure to keep the leaves wet. In order to insure this moisture,

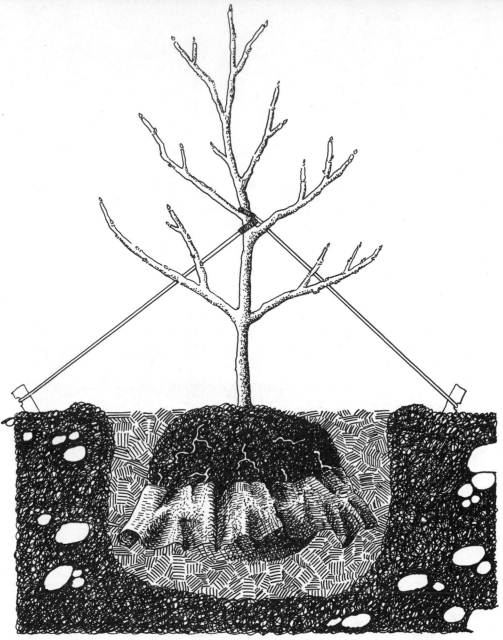

Planting a balled and burlaped tree. Note that the hole is huge and that the burlap, though pulled back from the trunk is left on to hold the ball firmly. It will rot with time. And, at the top of the tree, guy wires are attached to hold the tree in the wind until the roots do the job. The tree itself is protected from these wires by 8 inch sections of garden hose.

you may have to spray it several times a day for a while. You definitely should shade your new plant for at least a month, allowing it only indirect sun. Cheesecloth does the trick if you're handy about making tents or awnings and the like.

Many people use both polyethylene and cheesecloth in their awning, letting it dangle almost to the ground to hold a great deal of added moisture in the immediate area of the plant. Don't prolong polyethylene protection though. Too much moisture, concentrated too long, promotes mildew or fungus.

It takes a full month of spring growing for your plant to become reasonably settled. During that time it should be shaded, watered and *not* fed. Fertilizers of any kind can prove damaging at this point. Wait a couple of months. After a month of almost absurd care, you should gradually reduce the amount of shade your plant is receiving. New roots will have formed and the supply of water to the leaves should be able to handle their evaporation. But ease it into the sun. Too much sets you back. Too little reduces the production of the leaves and so makes additional root growing more difficult. In short, when it comes to food and sun, force only that activity on the plant that it can handle. But make every effort to keep both leaves and roots moist.

That Apple Sapling

Remember that sapling in the wall? Well, out of pride but under the guise of education, I would like to explain the fiendishly-ingenious technique employed in transplanting it.

One sunny afternoon in the fall, I dismantled much of that stone wall. I removed every stone that didn't contain some pocket of soil on which the tree relied. After fiddling around quite awhile, I decided to build a kind of bucket of stone around the thing. I then cut the tree's two largest roots, leaving three or so smaller ones wandering all over the stone wall. I coated the cut ends of the roots with rooting hormone and made two or three small slices in the root and applied hormone there, too. The stone bucket was filled with a magnificent mixture of soil, sand, vermiculite and leaf mold. I watered all this good stuff and went away.

By the following September, the damn thing had grown more than it had in an entire lifetime of struggling. It was substantially out of proportion and not at all like the twisted sapling I had wanted. So I pruned it back and cut a couple of other roots. I watered all this good stuff and went away.

Two years after my first visit, I returned to my little tree and dug it up. It was an easy process, actually, since the soil I had supplied was loaded with vigorous roots. I planted the thing,

protected it and cared for it like a mother hen. And I was repaid
with a tree that grew so hearty that I'm now doomed to constant
pruning, both of its roots and top growth, to keep it under even
minimal control.

P.S. I rebuilt the wall.

Seedlings

The digging of seedlings, I've discovered, isn't a common
pastime. In fact, dedicated seedling hunters are few and far between.
But the rarity of those who partake of this particular form of plant
piratage (piratage?) can be explained as a result of their ignorance.
In short, most people don't think of it. But I do, all the time. And I
do so for a complex set of reasons that make perfect sense to me and
do, I trust, to anyone whose gardening interests overreach his
purchasing power.

So that the impoverished among us may carry on this
conversation without a hint of embarrassment or the threat that
someone will inform American Express that we lied about our
incomes, I would like to ask all you rich people to leave the room.
Thank you.

Now then, both wild and garden-variety seedlings are growing
everywhere. They are the natural products of healthy, fertile plants
and sprout all the time. In a garden, such seedlings are called
volunteers, a name that has mixed connotations. For the landed
gentleman with a well-established scheme of shrubs and trees and no
shortage of funds to limit his landscaping, a volunteer is a weed. It
grows where things aren't supposed to grow, or where something
else is trying to. And, as a result, volunteers are weeded out.

In the wild or semi-wild, volunteers are just seedlings. But, they
are nonetheless doomed. With very few exceptions, seedlings
growing in forests are killed by the high shade of adult trees. Or
they start growth in places that can't for long support them. Of
course, some make it and grow into huge trees. But most of the
seeds that fall naturally never germinate and much of what makes it
that far, goes no further.

Basically, then, the expeditionary fool has a terrific source of free
plants. The gardener in search of little-known varieties of shrub and
tree can offer his services to any large property holder and feel
reasonably certain that a day of weeding will yield him a ton of stuff

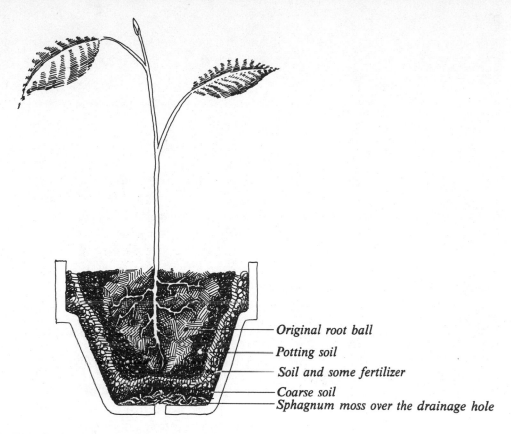

Original root ball
Potting soil
Soil and some fertilizer
Coarse soil
Sphagnum moss over the drainage hole

The ideal potting procedure for seedlings.

well-worth the effort. And these will come from both nature and his
garden.

There are only two major considerations to the digging of
seedlings that you should know about. The first is potentially the
most disappointing. It involves the curious and nasty habit of most
hybrid plants to produce offspring that bear only the faintest
resemblance to their parents. Generally, fruit trees and ornamentals,
such as twisted varieties of split leaf maple, produce seeds that have
an almost random genetic makeup. And so the trees produced look
like almost anything, at random. Before bothering with such a plant,
you should identify it and look it up in an encyclopedia of plants. A
good one (often recommended in this book and worth the high cost)
tells you what propagating methods are suitable to a particular plant.
You may find that cuttings are recommended and that either seeds
are not mentioned at all or are specifically ruled out. In such a case,
of course, follow the directions if you are strictly interested in the
parent type.

Wild seedlings almost always grow true to type. That is, they
look like their parents. But there are exceptions. Diseased and
mutant branches of wild trees sometimes produce seeds. Many of the
most unusual varieties of shrubs and ornamentals have been

gathered by horticulturalists from this weird source and then grown. Many of these seedlings end up useless or dead, but some turn out to have a quirk of character that is especially beautiful and so are propagated. But that's only a sort of aside. And you should know that the odds are astronomically against your finding such a bunch of seedlings and even more remote of having any real success with them. The point that this paragraph started out to make is that seedlings growing in the wild grow huge. Unless contained by the dwarfing methods of bonsai practice, they quickly become very un-cute. That lovely seedling can get big fast.

I can't let this opportunity go by without taking advantage of it. I have only recently become smitten with the art of bonsai. I've long admired the things but have just now started trying my hand. And I think that a pirated seedling may well be the ideal opportunity for you to try as well. You can control its growth and train it as you go, if you like. At any rate, bonsai offers a set of skills that I'm sure you will admire and many of them will certainly prove useful. When I get interested in a subject, I buy too many books about it and read them all. I've just come off such a binge and so I now offer one of the rare plugs to be found in this book. Ann Kimball Pipe has written a book called *Bonsai: The Art of Dwarfing Trees* (Hawthorn) and George F. Hull one called *Bonsai For Americans* (Doubleday). They are both excellent. I suggest you buy them. Even if you never grow a dwarfed tree, you will learn something about plants that you might not anywhere else. A remarkably lovely form of gardening. I'm awed by it.

As to specific instructions concerning the transplanting of seedlings, I'm happy to say that there is very little to know. Gathering a root ball with nearly all of the seedling's roots in it isn't very hard to do. However, you should still show the plant the respect due a transplant and keep it moist, shaded and out of the wind for a month or so. All the rules that apply to large transplants work here as well, but you don't have to be so worried about it.

Cuttings

Most horticulturalists and experienced gardeners tell you (ad nauseum) that successful cuttings are dependent on the proper choice of species, the correct timing of the cutting and the treatment that they receive after being cut. And they're right, in their way, of course. These are precisely the factors involved insofar as the success of the *cuttings* are concerned. These are just the influences that will determine whether a large percentage of your cuttings live or die. But neither you nor I makes his living by increasing the percentage of rooted cuttings in any one batch we try. Rather, we go at it for the fun of trying and a few successes. We maintain and hold our sense of good times and, in so doing, preserve our sanity by playing in the dirt with leaves and twigs.

I hope you see the difference. My book and I are much more interested in successful *cutters* than successful cuttings. In time you'll probably get addicted to the thing, go crazy trying to do it all better and more effectively. You'll start to keep a diary of cuttings, rooting mediums, time, light, success proportions and the like. It's perfectly understandable for a normal, healthy person to become fanatical about something perfectly beautiful and harmless in a world so perfectly full of harm. Don't be surprised if you find that there is very little that you've done that you are so ridiculously proud of as you are of your rooted split leaf maple. But don't wreck it by figuring out what percentage of your maple cuttings died. For God's sake.

I've managed to blither through mountains of cuttings, devastating (if I had counted) thousands of them by too little or too much water or the wrong timing. But until I sat down to write about cuttings, I'd never considered it that way. Basically, if I manage a success now and then, I feel perfectly justified in ignoring my defeats. Mostly, that's my bent of mind. Seeing one little bugger set roots and thrive is such a triumphal event to me that I can't at all be bothered with the mitigating circumstances that nine died. Clearly, that's no way to run a country or a war or a large corporation, but I'm not, I'm playing in the dirt. I take great glee in it and compensate for my inadequacies with a little guile. I'll explain later how to up your chances. But right now I'd like to say that you shouldn't worry about it too much. Remember always that a cutting usually comes from something that was too big anyway and that one success is one more than you had any right to expect.

It's hard to write a book on successful plant propagation when you openly admit that 'success' isn't the most important part of propagation. And, it's even more difficult to teach people to do something while telling them they have no right to expect it to work. But, in my last paragraph that's just what I did. With that advice I find myself on the verge of a problem. Writers often come to problems like this, I guess, but that doesn't make it any easier for me. Nevertheless, I'm going to blunder right through so that you'll understand the way I feel about propagating plants.

Most people don't feel much of anything about propagating plants. They either do it or they don't. They're either good at it or they aren't. But I've done so much of it that I've had lots of time and quiet to think about the whole business while I was mucking around in rooting mediums with the severed limbs of bushes, trees and plants. And so I've drawn some conclusions from both their ability to survive and my propensity to be amazed by their survival. And if I write a couple of paragraphs about being awed by plant life I'm going to start sounding like a guy with three beers under his belt after having attended a Sierra Club lecture on the smog threat to cactus and wild succulents. And I don't want to sound like a Sierra Club lecture. I don't look at things quite that way. So please bear with me while I try to make this into my sort of explanation.

In the first place, man didn't think up propagation. Nature, in all her wonder, transplanted things by flood, distributed seed by animal and wind and even floated cuttings to other sites long before we started fooling around with the same techniques. And, like a good Darwinian, I assume that there have been ages of selection in favor of those plants that are capable of easy propagation, both sexual (by seed or spore) and asexual (by the generation of a new plant from a part of an old one, other than a seed or spore). I understand that there is nothing magical about the ability of cells to differentiate into roots even though they originated in a leafy cutting. But I am amazed by it.

And I think that it's important to be amazed. I think that it's fine to study the world and take advantage of what it has to offer. I think it's only sensible of man to try and get nature to do what he wants it to. But I think that we ought to keep being stunned a little by it all. Even as we exploit to one degree or another the natural propensities of plants to do what we want, I think that we ought to be boggled by the intricacy of the process. I think that if we remember this and honestly feel impressed by the natural world, then we won't be so quick to discard or abuse or pervert what's going on in it. And I know that that's a large conclusion to draw from a small cutting. But it's important to respect the wonderfulness of it. So please don't assume that a hunk of bush will dance automatically to your whims and generate roots when stuck in moist perlite. The chances are very good that it will do just that, but be amazed anyway. That's all I have to say about it.

This chapter is about those kinds of asexual propagation that I lump under the heading of 'cuttings.' That, to me, means the removal of an above-ground part of a plant and its transportation to another place where it is encouraged to generate its own root system. The marvel of this process involves the production of root cells by leaf or stem cells. The knowledge of what a root cell is like is locked up in a leaf cell and, under the right conditions, the leaf or stem or bud can be allowed to remember and then produce roots. That's really nifty.

Gardeners use this method of producing plants for several reasons. Quantity is not one of them. By far the fastest way to produce a great number of plants is to sow seeds. Literally tens of thousands of plants can be grown from one adult in a matter of a few seasons. But sowing seeds has limitations for the gardener.

Many of the hybrids that have been developed are sterile. They are beautiful, hardy, resistent to disease and doomed if they have to rely on seeds for their population growth. So the gardeners who have developed these hybrids propagate them by cuttings.

Other hybrids aren't sterile but nevertheless show odd tendencies in their seeds. They don't grow 'true to type.' That is, the seed won't produce an adult like the parent. Maples are notorious in this regard. Some of the most beautifully-twisting split leaf ornamentals produce seed that create straight trees. Such plants must be reproduced by cuttings in order to retain many of the qualities that make them valuable.

And even some cuttings don't produce true to type. Sansevieria, for instance, produce offspring by leaf cuttings that lack the characteristic striping of the parent. And there are a few rare cases in which flowering pink plants produce white flowers on rooted leaves and red ones on plants grown from root cuttings. However amazing these exceptions are, they are equally rare. Most plants produce an exact replica of the parent's characteristics if propagated by means of cuttings.

By the way, any form of asexual reproduction can't actually be considered a parent-child relationship. In fact, the offspring is a continuation of the original, not a new 'generation' in the sexual sense. Thus, plants that are propagated asexually belong to something called a 'clone,' or single individual, that has been divided into more than one plant. Cloning involves not only the use of cuttings but also of division, grafting, budding and any means of producing new plants from an original without the use of seeds or spores.

Soil and Other Mediums

Before discussing the various kinds of cuttings and the ways of rooting them, I think that some information about soil and rooting mediums is in order. From explanations that have come before, you should know that cuttings can generate roots if they have an environment that supplies them with the raw materials they need. The rooting medium is one very important aspect of that environment. So it will help you to understand how things root if you know what stuff they root in.

Sometimes it takes several weeks and even months to root a cutting from a plant. During that time it must be supplied with a number of things. The container in which you keep the cutting and the medium into which it is inserted supply almost all of what it needs. Obviously, then, the container and medium are pretty important.

Regardless of whether you are sticking your twigs in pots, Skippy jars, flats or cold frames, it's important that they be held firmly in place for the duration and not fall over. So the medium must be firm and dense enough and hold its shape.

Your cutting also needs a ready supply of water. So the medium should hold water, but not so much as to soak. The medium should be, in the obscure language of the gardener, 'moist' not wet. To my knowledge, no one has ever committed to print a concrete description of the distinction between moist and wet. In a solemn effort to produce a first, I will now try. Beware in advance, however, that you are likely to be disappointed. Dry means substantially without water. None. Wet means soaked, loaded with water or having so much that there is very little air in the medium. Moist means having enough water so that your plants or cuttings don't die and enough air below the surface so that they don't drown or rot. Moist then is the condition between dry and wet. The definitive borderline between moist and wet is marked by the survival of your cuttings. Disappointed? I'll try some more. But it's only going to get more confusing.

It's not surprising that cuttings need air. Almost everything else does. But it is sometimes difficult, or at least inconvenient, to see that they get both air and water. In order to ensure both, mediums are chosen and mixed with an eye to the balance of air and water.

The first consideration is their ability to hold water within themselves. But, to add to the confusion, mediums hold water in two ways. Sand holds water on its surface by surface tension. The smaller the grains of sand, the more surface area to it per cubic inch. So, the more water it can hold. Hence, soil or mediums that have small grains are called 'heavy.' They hold more water and are, indeed, heavier. Such heavy mediums hold so much water that they have little room for air. Larger grains of sand have larger air spaces between them and hold less water by surface tension. The other method of holding water is by absorption. Peat moss, sphagnum moss, perlite, vermiculite and other such materials soak up water into themselves. They hold considerable amounts for long periods of time. As anything around these materials dries out, they exude water to equalize its concentration in the medium.

The amount of water that a medium holds has a great deal to do with how much air it can hold as well. Describing water retention, drainage and porosity is a kind of redundant task. All three are closely linked to each other. But, a porous substance can hold both air and water if it absorbs the water. And a thing can drain well and still have ample water in it. The point is that a porous mixture has airspaces in it and, regardless of whether it absorbs water, it holds that air for your cuttings.

For convenience, most mediums are contrived so that they absorb and hold water over a long period. This simply makes it possible to ignore cuttings longer while they are rooting. But, in order to ensure good drainage, a certain amount of porous material is added and, in order to hold cuttings vertical and in place while they root, some dense, heavy stuff is included. Thus, you end up with mixtures like peat moss and sand. Or perlite and granite chips. Or sphagnum and sand. A brief description of each element may help you to decide what to choose. And then, in case you've chosen wrong, I'll tell you what works for me.

Perlite is a volcanic ash that, oddly, doesn't absorb water very readily but holds tremendous quantities of it once soaked. If used alone, it simply floats. So it must be mixed with a heavier material.

Vermiculite is expanded mica. It absorbs water a bit more readily than perlite but doesn't hold quite so much of it.

Sphagnum moss is a moss grown in bogs. It can be bought either milled or coarse but should be broken up rather finely for rooting mediums. Sphagnum holds water so well that it can overload and so create too wet a medium. Many growers soak it for several hours and then squeeze all the water out of it that they can with their hands. This having been done, the sphagnum can rightfully be said to be in that magical condition known as 'moist.'

Peat moss is another variety of gunk, dredged from swamps, that absorbs water. Generally speaking, it is somewhat decomposed when bought. However, some varieties are more rotted than others. Those that are lighter in color are very acid. Those that are a dark chocolate-brown are more nearly neutral and more thoroughly decomposed and so are better for most rooting requirements. Peat moss absorbs slowly, especially if dry, and should be soaked and squeezed before being added to any medium. If peat moss dries out, it is very difficult to wet it again.

Sand is sand. But river sand is not beach sand because it is usually more coarse and contains no damaging salt. And you should buy specially-sterilized sand. Sand comes in a million different textures, but most of them tend to hold water very well and should be used with some other substance to ensure porosity.

Soil should be sterilized for use with cuttings. Most packaged potting soils are very heavy and will probably require some coarse material for drainage and air.

Granite chips are just what they sound like. Coarse and loaded with air space.

You can feel confident in using one part sand, one part perlite or moss and one part soil in making a rooting medium. This is a kind of all-purpose medium that works well for most seeds and plants as well. However, many people omit the use of soil altogether since it makes pulling the rooted cuttings out of their containers more difficult when it comes time to transplant. Many use nothing but vermiculite and sphagnum and swear by it. All this is pretty confusing, so, by volume, mix one part each of sand, sphagnum and perlite and use that until you feel like experimenting.

There's one other note on mediums that I should mention. Sphagnum moss has become a great favorite among gardeners because it is extremely resistant to a fungus called 'damping off.' This fungus has destroyed many cuttings since it grows readily in moist, confined areas. In order to control damping off disease, you can include sphagnum in your mixture and/or mince or grate it and spread some in a thin layer across the top of the medium. In general, because of its resistance to the fungi, sphagnum is preferable to peat moss.

And I should also note that different kinds of cuttings react very differently to various mediums. Where one sort roots very well in sand and peat moss, it grows much slower in sand, soil and leaf mold. Or the opposite may be true. Similarly, some cuttings prefer inert mediums like sand, perlite and vermiculite exclusively. Other than reading and experimenting, there is no simple way to clarify the problem beyond that. You should know, though, that most things will root if they're going to. That is, a change in medium may speed up or slow down the rooting but, as a rule, it won't prevent it if the basic requirements of any medium are met.

Sorry, there's one more, rather general point about rooting mediums that I should mention. Cuttings that are rooted in perlite or vermiculite or sand cannot draw any nutrients from them. There are simply none to be had. As a result, you should transplant them as soon as they have established roots substantial enough to be moved. You should then put them in a pot or in the ground so that they can begin to grow in earnest. Cuttings set in mixtures containing soil, however, can be left much longer without worrying about the plant's survival.

Putting Soil In Containers

Enormous amounts of apparently random opinion are bantered about concerning the ways in which soil should be applied to pot. This is true for plants, seedlings, seeds and cuttings. But insofar as the pirating of cuttings is concerned, you need only consider the same variables that went into the choice of a mixture. In order to ensure appreciable moisture, you should pack the very bottom layer of medium rather firmly. In order to allow good air space and drainage, you should push lightly on the top layer of soil. At the time of inserting a cutting, though, you should push the soil into solid contact with the stem so that moisture is always available. The details of insertion are handled more thoroughly a little later on.

As I mentioned at the beginning of this chapter, the most important variables in rooting cuttings are the selection of the plant, the treatment it receives and the time of the cutting. 'Time' here means a couple of things. First it means the time of day, although this is of relatively less importance. The critical time element is the 'season' or point in the cycle of growth that you choose. This isn't especially important in the case of house plants but where outdoor plants are concerned, it is crucial. In fact, the three major types of cuttings for outdoor plants are distinguished by the point in their cycle when cut.

Softwood Cuttings

The use of the term 'softwood' here is somewhat deceptive. In fact, I object to it even as I perpetuate the convention. But I'm also going to be quick to qualify its use. Generally, softwood cuttings are taken from the current year's growth of a tree or shrub shortly after that growth has begun to mature. The wood of the cutting, then, isn't really 'soft.' It should have darkened somewhat from its original light color and the stem of the cutting should be stiff but not brittle. The point at which such a cutting is mature enough varies from species to species. But some understanding of the requirements of such a cutting may help.

The severed new growth is going to have to subsist on its own stored water and nutrients for as long as it takes for the cutting to produce roots. There are many things that can be done to make that survival easier but the few leaves and a stem have to make it on their own for some time. Thus, very immature growth, that would be making considerable demands for food stuffs and water if left alone, stand a slimmer chance of weathering the difficulties. On the other hand, the older the growth, the slower it is to produce roots.

Simplified (and with a great, tiresome amount of discussion on cell division omitted), this means you should choose your softwood cuttings when they seem ready to stand on their own but while they are still slightly adolescent.

Another consideration in this timing business is the general need to root and establish the plant before winter. Deciduous plants lose their leaves in the winter and, once they have done so, have only the remotest chance of rooting. The idea then is to root them, allow them to mature and 'harden' and then put them outside in a protected place to go through the aggravations of winter so that they can rejoin their normal cycles in the spring.

There's one other quite arbitrary distinction to make here. Evergreen softwood cuttings are treated very differently from deciduous cuttings. So, in order to keep them quite separate in your mind, I'm not dealing with evergreen cuttings here at all. Later on you'll find a section called 'Winter Cuttings.' These are softwood cuttings from evergreens.

Now then, sometime in the late spring or early summer, you'll cut a piece from a deciduous shrub or tree. You'll almost reflexively worry that you're being impatient and that it's too soon. It may be. Don't worry about it. Cut only about one third as many pieces as you want and wait a week. Cut some more. Wait another week. Cut some more. This is called the shotgun approach to unscientific softwood cuttings. If everything else is as it should be, one of the batches will be right. If everything else is as it should be, all three will probably root pretty well. Anyway, the odds are with you.

I mentioned before that the time of day for taking cuttings makes a difference. I bring it up now since there is a ritual I've borrowed from the Japanese that has both emotional satisfactions and horticultural advantages for making cuttings succeed. I've found that

I am very bad at doing those things that pure reason suggests, even though I am invariably disappointed when I don't. So I habitually develop fantastic reasons for sensible actions. I somehow take perverse pleasure in making things work for the wrong reasons. Taking cuttings is one such ritual.

The Japanese first became interested in dwarfed trees growing naturally and later refined the dwarfing process into the art of bonsai. The interrelation between natural and cultivated dwarfs, however, has remained and many fine bonsai specimens are plants gathered from the wild. Such gathered plants have always been valued and a class of nurserymen developed in Japan to hunt for and collect these specimens. For many reasons, such plants are fragile and very difficult to transplant successfully. (See *Expeditions*) However, the Japanese collector created a ritual of journeying into the mountains and camping there for the night while meditating on the next day's task. Doing so must have been a tiring business, camping not having then risen to the state of luxurious vacation it now enjoys. And everyone knows that a long evening's meditation can put you to sleep about as fast as anything. The result, of course, is waking up early, all-meditated and raring to go.

My adaptation of this ritual involves the contemplation and care, during the entire previous day, of the plant I intend to pirate. What I mean is that I water it thoroughly. The plant likes that and I figure it will be good to me as a result. We make friends and talk a little. That's the meditation part. And, in form if not detail similar to the Japanese gardener, I get up early, feel raring to go and make my cuttings early in the morning. I go through this process with every kind of propagation—cuttings of leaves, roots, stems, division, grafting, even transplanting. And, having appeased the spirit of the plant with my concern, it usually smiles on me and my endeavor.

The ritual is lovely in itself, especially if you like plants. It makes me feel better both about dismembering the parent and the time and effort that goes into the chance of the cuttings rooting.

I've been told that the spirit of the plant is unmoved by my ministrations. Sceptics of every variety have explained that my ritual is successful because the day-long watering fills the cuttings with moisture so that they are as strong as possible when cut. I've also heard that the cool, shady, early morning is ideal for maintaining the stiff, turgid state of my cuttings and that, thus, they stand the best chance of enduring and rooting if taken at this time. The spirit of both plant and pirate ignore such logic, however, and rest secure in the knowledge that the humours that flow through the veins of plants are vivified by a lightness of heart and early morning dew.

The Cutting

The most important threat to a cutting is that of drying out before roots have formed. In order to limit that threat, many methods of retaining water and hastening root development are used by gardeners. However, the evaporation of water from a cutting is a simple process and even the most poorly equipped of propagators

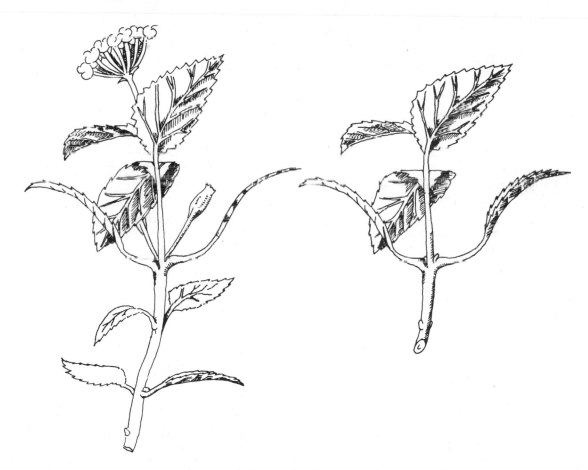

Reducing a cutting to its strongest parts. Flowers, seed pods, weak leaves and excess stem are removed and the base is cut at an angle a quarter inch or so below a node. Lopping off the weaklings leaves a stronger whole.

can substantially limit that loss. The most important step is in the preparation of the cutting.

Plants lose water through their leaves. Not only do they use it in the photosynthetic process but they breath it, or sweat it, as well. The drier the air around the plant and the more sun that falls on it, the more water that is lost. The other variable in this water-loss equation is the surface area of the leaves. The more leaves, the more surface area and the more water loss. Simple. So, basically, cuttings should be small. They should have a few healthy leaves, no flowers and several buds.

Most cuttings are from four to six inches long. The bottom one third to one half of the leaves are removed and any flower stems, forming seeds and unhealthy leaves are taken off as well. The cutting is removed from the plant with a 45 degree angled cut made about one half of an inch from a node. That last bit of instruction isn't as arbitrary as it sounds. The angled cut is made so that when the cutting is stuck into the medium, the base of it has a large surface area to suck in water and also so that it won't be sitting flat. The angled cut reduces the possibility of rotting. The business about the node is equally sensible. Nodes are the places on a stem where a leaf or bud is located. It is these areas where substantial growth occurs. So nodes are most likely to produce roots. The half-inch cut below the node simply protects it from damage and drying out.

Many very large-leafed plants have too much leaf area for long-term rooting. In these cases, you can remove part of a leaf. Cut it with a very sharp, clean razor.

Absolutely immediately after you have made a cutting, stuff it into a plastic bag that is wet inside. The wetter the cuttings stay, the less of their own moisture they will lose. And since holding moisture in the cutting is the point and challenge of almost everything that is to follow, you might as well start right away.

Generally, cuttings taken from the ends of branches, called terminal cuttings, are the most successful. However, there's no reason to discard pieces taken from lower on the stem if pruning them is necessary. Try everything.

Hormones

In the last ten years, there have been some significant developments in the fine arts of plant growth and care. The rooting

of cuttings has consumed a great deal of the energies of those who run commercial nurseries, since so many new hybrids require this sort of reproduction. At the end of this litany of rooting methods, there are discussions of propagating equipment and techniques that are extremely helpful. But this, I think, is the place for a short discussion of the wonder stuff of the rooting freak: rooting hormone.

The most common hormone, called IBA (actually indolebutyric acid), is sold almost everywhere. It comes in extremely diluted concentrations of from .1% to .8% mixed with talc. Thus, it is a powder. Many brands of hormone come with a small amount of fungicide mixed with them for obvious reasons. And, if you have some extremely difficult project in mind, you can ask your local nursery for a stronger concentration of the stuff, up to 2%.

Simply put, rooting hormones 'instruct' cells in the process of transforming themselves into roots. In so doing, they have made it possible to root in weeks plants that once took months and also to root species and varieties that once had to be grafted.

Planting

After your cutting has been collected, trimmed and readied for the rooting medium, you simply stick the bottom of the stem in water, shake off the excess and then dip the stem in the powdered hormone. Shake off the clumps of extra hormone and then stick the cutting in the rooting medium. That's that.

In cases where you suspect some resistance to rooting, you can further encourage it by making small slices in the stem where it is expected to root. Don't cut through the cambium layer (the light colored, fleshy stuff just underneath the bark), just cut to it. Then coat these cuts with hormone.

If you think that your rooting medium is a bit on the 'heavy,' wet side, you might try improving the drainage in the area of the cutting's base. Take a pencil or stick and drive a hole into the medium for the cutting. Then, before inserting it, pour a bit of coarse sand into the hole. Leave about an inch or two of hole unfilled and then insert the cutting. With your fingers, pinch the soil around the cutting against it. Make sure that the stem is in contact

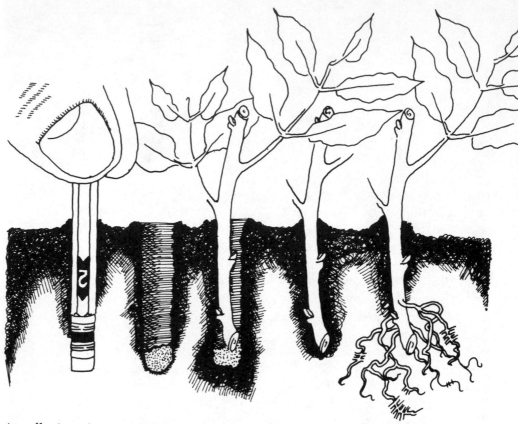

Actually, inserting a cutting is an easier business than explanations of how to do it imply. But what can you do? Explain simply, I guess. First, stick a pencil in the medium. Fill the bottom of the hole with sand (for drainage). Then, slide the cutting into the hole. Firm the soil around the stem so that it touches the stem, supply it with moisture and then wait.

with the medium at several points so that moisture is easily available to it.

I've been told and have also read that cuttings should be inserted into the medium at an angle. I've never, though, heard a convincing argument for this technique and find that those I stand at attention do as well as those that lounge a bit. You can try it any way you'd like.

Hardwood Cuttings.

Hardwood cuttings are a more or less specialized form of propagation. Generally, the technique is used to produce large amounts of something, such as in hedges or windbreaks, when money is a major issue.

Hardwood cuttings are made from deciduous plants shortly after the leaves have fallen. They are almost always from the current year's growth since these are the most likely to be successful. These cuttings aren't necessarily terminal growth and, in the assembly-line approach that usually befalls hardwood procedure, a great amount of wood is often chopped up in any number of ways. In the end, however, you should have a pile of sticks all about six to eight inches long. Each should have three or four nodes and the topmost bud should be about an inch from the end of the cutting.

Here comes the curious part of the technique. The cuttings are bundled with string, buried in slightly-moist sand and refrigerated. They should be kept at about 50 degrees F for about a month. During this time, the cut ends of the sticks form calluses and thus seal themselves from further moisture loss. But, since these cuttings are both hardwood and dormant, they are not especially susceptible to drying out.

After a month or so of 50 degree temperatures, the cuttings are then further refrigerated to about 35° to 40° F. Note that this temperature is just *above* freezing. And then they are left until after the last frost in the spring.

Immediately after that last frost, the cuttings are taken from the refrigerator and buried in a trench with only the topmost bud sticking up above ground. Water and wait.

It's important that these cuttings be planted as soon as the arrival of spring allows. If left too long, they will spontaneously react to some sort of inner clock and begin to grow shoots, even in the refrigerator. Once this growth has begun, the chances of their rooting are considerably reduced.

Most hardwood cuttings are made in hedge and fast-growing windbreak material such as Jasmine, Poplar or Willow. If carefully prepared and treated, you can hope for but rarely achieve a 75% success rate. (I mention the bugaboo of a percentage here since 75% of a hedge can look a little weird. As a result you should plant hardwood close together so that failures are filled in.)

As you may be able to tell from my cavalier treatment of hardwood cuttings, I haven't too much interest or experience in the method. I am not a commercial nursery and have never had occasion to install a hedge. However, I was once piqued by the idea of refrigerating sticks and so gave the process a try.

I decided, after several inquiries, to try a fig tree. Actually, having a firm grip and realistic idea of my own abilities, I tried two

Hardwood cuttings are made in the fall.

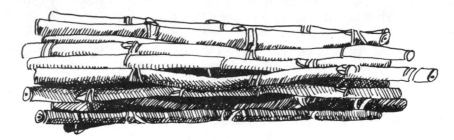

Eight inch or so sections are cooled (behind the garage under a few inches of sand) for a couple of months. Later, the cuttings are almost, but not quite, frozen until spring.

The cuttings are buried in the early spring with only one bud above ground. With water and luck as many as 60–70% may make it. (Note that my illustration is more optimistic than that.)

dozen of them. I made the cuttings, bound and half-buried them in the shade of my garage and waited a month. When I exhumed the things, they had, to my surprise, callused magnificently. So I buried them in a Tuperware box filled with moist sawdust and put them in the refrigerator. In the spring they were planted in a barrel. An above ground container warms quickly, I reasoned, and so would give my cuttings all the help they needed.

Six rooted. Huzzah!

Now, for those of you who have no need for six or even more fig trees but are still curious about hardwood cuttings, I have some terrific news. In the fall I cut the whips back very hard. After waiting a few weeks for them to recover from this shock, I transplanted one to my own property and gave the other five away (actually, I gave four away and swapped the last for a dozen cuttings from a coveted umbrella pine). All but one came on strong the following spring. And they've been doing beautifully ever since. I'm not enough of an expert in such matters to know if the transplanting of hardwood cuttings is a common enterprise. But at least now you know that it can be done.

Winter Cuttings

I've a confession to make. Given the way I've been running off at the mouth in this book, it should come as no great surprise to you. But I think that it's only fair that I point out my natural biases as we go along so that my liquid prose won't take you unaware and insidiously incline you to only a few forms of plant pirating. I would hate to wake up later and find that I had implicitly emphasized and glorified one form of rooting cuttings over another. That truly would be journalistic irresponsibility. So, to counter my proclivities, I would like to here state quite explicitly that I am unduly enamoured of evergreens and their propagation. In fact, I'm nuts about them.

What I really like, of course, is producing the things. And, since I am not a wealthy man, I have only a little ground on which to plant them once they've rooted. In self-defense I've taken to propagating natural and hybrid dwarfs of almost everything I can get my hands on, especially evergreens. Evergreens, you see, are small, dense, stay lovely year round and give me something to do in the winter. So, here is my bit on evergreens.

Winter cuttings are taken from evergreens almost exactly as

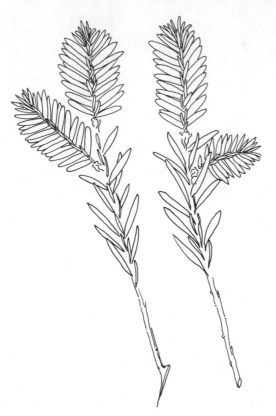

The evergreen cutting to the left has a "heel." It has been torn from the tree. The one on the right has been cut off cleanly.

softwood cuttings are taken from deciduous trees and shrubs. The only difference is that the cuttings are made at any time from October to December. Some four to six inches of growth is cut and the lower one third of the cutting is stripped of needles. In cases such as my dwarf, needled evergreens, where a six inch piece may constitute a substantial part of the plant, as little as one to two inches may be used.

The matter of removing the cutting from the plant is another of those areas where there seems to be disagreement. Many evergreen propagators swear that taking a 'heel' with the cutting leads to a greater proportion of success. Others think this is nonsense. I don't know. Anyway, taking a heel is a simple matter of pulling rather than cutting a piece off. In so doing, you tear the bark and some cambium from the parent plant in the shape of a foot (hence the name). Most modern authorities on propagation now simply take the noncommittal and, therefore, cowardly approach of citing but not recommending either method. That is exactly what I'm going to do too. But, you should probably try both and take a count of your successes with each method, if for no other reason than to have an opinion on the subject.

Use hormone and rooting mediums on evergreens as you would on any other softwood cutting.

Since winter cuttings are made in the winter (hence the name), they must be protected in one way or another from freezing. The

A cutting of Umbrella pine.

standard procedure is to put them in a cold frame with an insulation of hay or grass around them. During very cold periods, the covering of the frame may be further insulated.

Since most of you probably don't have cold frames, you can either read later on about how to make one or improvise your treatment of the cuttings. The cold frame is used in order to force the cuttings through the normal cycle of a winter without subjecting them to the rigors of freezing temperatures. Ideally, they should stay at about 40 to 50° F. Lacking the means of maintaining that sort of temperature, you can put them on an enclosed porch or on the window sill of your garage until the weather gets too cold. Then, move them inside where they can get a healthy amount of sun. Put them away from the heat and on the floor, if possible. Once the threat of freezing temperatures has passed, move them back outdoors.

The important point here is that too much warmth damages winter cuttings. By May or June they will have rooted and can be transplanted.

I find evergreen cuttings a great pleasure. Slow-growing ones are especially attractive gifts as quasi-Mame bonsai. You'll have to hunt around some for the proper pots but, once you find them, you're likely to become very interested in growing these fragile miniatures in their thimble of soil. Beware though. Mame bonsai require almost perfect conditions to thrive and, if you would like to offer these or

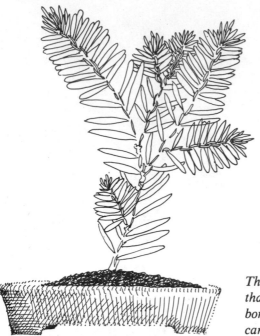

This is a rooted evergreen cutting that has been potted in the Mame bonsai style. Small pots like this one can be had at most large nurseries.

any other rooted cuttings as gifts, you might be better off buying the tiny seed pots available at most nurseries. These allow direct planting in the soil without actually transplanting.

Cuttings in Water

There are very few outdoor plants that really prefer propagation in water alone. There are those that don't mind it. Sort of a take-it-or-leave-it reaction might best characterize their preferences. But, generally, water alone doesn't supply ideal conditions.

But a great many plants grow roots in water. Your degree of success is slightly lowered and the range of plants that work is reduced, but you might as well try it since it is so easy and will probably pique your interest enough to get you involved in pirating on a larger scale.

Indoor plants, though, often react much better when dumped in a glass of water. Many strike root and thrive with almost no concern on your part for their well-being.

Stem Cuttings of Indoor Plants

Plants like Wandering Jew, Begonia and almost any ivy root quickly in water. All you need do is cut a bit of stem exactly as you would a softwood cutting, one-half inch below a node, and remove any excess leaves. There's almost nothing to it. Use a tall glass, one that almost completely surrounds the entire cutting, and fill it one-third full. The surrounding glass helps keep the air around the cutting moist and so reduce water loss.

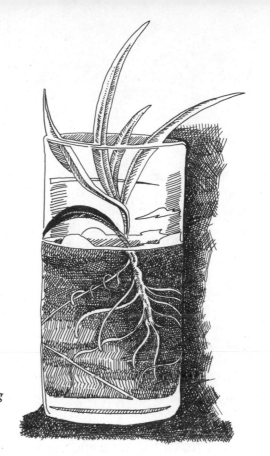

A cutting in water. Keeping the cutting low in a glass holds some moisture in the air around the leaves.

Crowns

Another stem configuration that often roots in water is that of the 'crown.' A crown is a ground-level node from which a spray of stems and leaves projects. Many plants, such as African Violet, look and flower best if each plant contains only one crown. However, African Violets often produce several.

It's relatively easy to take a knife and separate the extra crowns from the main plant. You should look over the crown carefully to check for fungus because most are susceptible to some form of infection. If you come across any fungi, remove as much of it as you can with a knife and coat what remains with fungicide. (In such a case, you should use a rooting medium of perlite rather than water only to avoid washing the fungicide from direct contact with the infected parts.) However, if the crown is healthy, it takes only a couple of weeks to root it. Just prop it in a shallow dish of water and keep it out of direct sunlight.

Other Indoor Plant Methods

Water is certainly the simplest way of propagating cuttings. But it isn't nearly as effective as the use of a medium that allows both air and water to reach the stem. As a result, many indoor plants are propagated outdoors in July and August. They are cut as are softwood cuttings and are tucked out of the way in a sandy area of the garden. Since most root very quickly, there's almost never any problem with the coming of cool weather.

You can, of course, also use pots or flats to propagate stem cuttings either indoors or out. All you need to remember is to keep them moist and away from very strong sunlight.

In General

In general, there is very little difference between the rooting of outdoor softwood cuttings and indoor stem cuttings. They are treated very similarly and nearly every technique applying to one works as well on the other. The next chapter deals with a variety of containers and other methods of rooting cuttings. If you are an indoor gardener, re-read the prior softwood cutting sections and think 'indoors' to yourself periodically. Then read about mediums and containers intoning the same word solemnly. The similarities in plants make the advice applicable.

There is one caution, however, that I should offer. It revolves around the pattern of growth in indoor plants that is much more obvious outdoors. Inside, you may be tempted to think of your plants as simply growing, without periods of rapid spurts or very marked degrees of maturity in the stems. Nope. Indoor plants grow like anything else and so the timing of the cutting is important with them as well.

August is a likely month for taking indoor cuttings. July works too. To check this timing simply break the stem of the plant instead of cutting it. If it snaps cleanly after bending a bit and then hangs from a thread of stringy outer covering, it is probably perfect. Stems that crush are too old, those that seem to be able to bend and never break are too young. And pick cuttings that are attractive. The quality and health of the cutting affects the quality and health of the rooted plant throughout its entire life.

Leaf Cuttings

Leaf cuttings and their propagation are among the plant marvels most strange and wonderful to me. Perhaps that's because most of the native North American plants with which I'm familiar are incapable of propagating themselves in this way. Or maybe because I know that asexual propagation is a natural function but don't really believe it. For whatever reason, leaves that naturally and regularly grow stems and roots always strike me as both odd by nature and terrific in their pirating possibilities.

It makes perfect sense that Nature should have developed such a tidy and even facile means of spreading itself around. But I tend to think of propagating plants by means of their parts as a human function and find it odd that many plants do it all by themselves. They do though.

One of my favorites is a West Coast native called *Tolmiea Menziesi,* better known as the Pick-a-back plant. It's a low-growing flowering thing that has learned to crawl, in a way, sending out feet that root and grow new feet. It is among the easiest of all flowering plants to root and, as a result, I'm constantly rooting mine to give as gifts to unsuspecting friends.

The Pick-a-back spreads naturally by growing entirely new plants from the center vein of its large mature leaves. As each leaf grows and spreads, its weight drops it to the ground where it roots and regrows. Plants capable of this sort of self-propagation are said to have 'viviparous' leaves, those that produce buds. Among the many house plants that produce buds on their leaves are the Kalanchoes, Sedums, and all manner of Water Lilies.

Rooting Leaves

If you have a plant that puts out large leaves that spontaneously sprout bunches of stems and leaves from their center veins, you can create a monster in almost no time. These things thrive on encouragement, as do you, and together you and your plant can become intoxicated with success. Shortly, and before you've had a chance to sober, you'll have a room filled with plants, all of which are producing plantlets at alarming rates. It is somehow a natural law of plant pirates and rooting freaks that you should attempt a large number of rarely successful and slow-rooting projects regularly. Concentrating on the easy ones isn't fair. Nor is it safe. You'll end up overrun.

But, under controlled circumstances and with a firm resolve and iron discipline, such plants are great. They serve as perfect safety valves for the impoverished gift giver. And they are spreaders of the propagating faith. I defy anyone to own a Pick-a-back or one of those things called 'Floppers' after the drooping habit of their leaves, and not root a leaf. And once someone has been successful with the exercise, he finds rooting like eating peanuts and ends up a fanatic. Giving someone such a plant is such a certain way of inducing the mania that it's almost cruel.

There are, in fact, two kinds of viviparous leaves: those that are enthusiastic and those that aren't. The enthusiastic ones continually generate leaves and extend themselves beyond their stems' ability to hold them all aloft. These are spontaneously viviparous. They naturally crawl and sprout. Rooting such a plant is easy. You simply put a small pot directly under a drooping leaf and wait for it to touch down and root. Or, you can cut the leaf from the parent plant and sit it firmly on a rooting medium. In a matter of days, most varieties of viviparous plants will root.

There are other kinds of viviparous plants as well. Perhaps the best known are the Begonias, African Violets and Peperomias. These don't have the maniacal spreading quality of those mentioned above and need a lot more encouragement.

Most of these plants produce buds and grow from a point at the base of their main leaf veins. Almost all Echeverias and Sedums can be propagated in this way. Simply pull a leaf off, being sure that you get all of the stem, and apply stem to rooting medium. Generally, those that both root and sprout from the base of the main vein are inserted in the medium vertically so that they look like lonely and stunted stem cuttings. The difference between stem cuttings and leaf cuttings is that the stem cuttings contain already existing buds where the leaves have to produce them.

I mentioned, I think, somewhere a few thousand words ago, that Sansevieria can be rooted from leaf cuttings. They are very easy, in fact, to propagate this way. You simply cut a leaf into a four to six inch piece and insert it in a moist medium. I single out Sansevieria at this point only because it is among those oddities of the propagating world that does not root true to type. Leaf cuttings of Sansevieria grow well enough but the strong yellow stripes of the parent are missing.

There is one other type of leaf cutting that is a lot of fun to play with. At least I find it curious. I always think that a rooting Begonia leaf is somehow a testament to the absurdly-persistent ability to survive that marks all of this book. But the Begonia is sort of

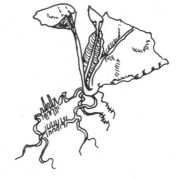

Begonia leaves will sprout plantlets from slices in their veins. Make razor cuts at the veins and put the leaf on a moist medium.

quintessentially enthusiastic about staying alive. And the way I root them typifies that.

Begonia leaves are viviparous. But not only do they produce roots and stems from the base of their main veins but they also sprout where the side veins are ruptured. This means that you can root several plants from one leaf. Simply remove one leaf from the plant, slice the veins of the leaf at several points from the underside and then set it in a moist rooting medium. Since it is important to keep the leaf in contact with the medium, many people use pins to tack it down. I, however, just drop a pebble in the middle of the leaf.

Before very long the Begonia will produce mini-plants where you have sliced into its veins. You can then take a razor to the leaf, separating the new plants and potting them individually.

Each plantlet can be potted separately.

Another approach to Begonia leaves is to go through this cutting up process in advance. You can literally hack up a leaf and put pieces of it on the medium for rooting.

Most fleshy leaves root. In fact, most of them are billed as being capable of producing stems and leaves anywhere you slice into their veins. African Violets are said to be capable of this. But I've found that most survive better if you plant the entire leaf intact without this kind of abuse. The Begonia is an exception and so much fun to watch explode with life that you ought to try it.

Leaf-Bud Rootings

Viviparous plants are capable of generating stem and roots where there were no buds. Most plants, of course, can't do this. But an enterprising horticulturalist found a way to root single leaves of Rhododendron by including a dormant bud with the leaf cutting.

The leaf is cut from the main branch with a razor or knife so that a heel of sorts is taken containing a bud. The leaf is then planted with rooting hormone in a moist medium. Time, care and a great deal of moisture surrounding the leaves will produce quite startling plants.

The original leaf never changes in these rootings. It simply provides the resources to produce the roots and then to stimulate the bud. The small plants that result are healthy and true to type. And all that from one bud.

Being something of a Rhodo lover, I've made several rootings this way. Not so much because it is easier than taking cuttings but because it is more impressive to get so much from such a little bud. And you can root dozens of plants from a single parent. Neat. I use a sand, vermiculite and peat moss medium that is heavy on the peat moss. I've made cuttings from both new and year old growth and

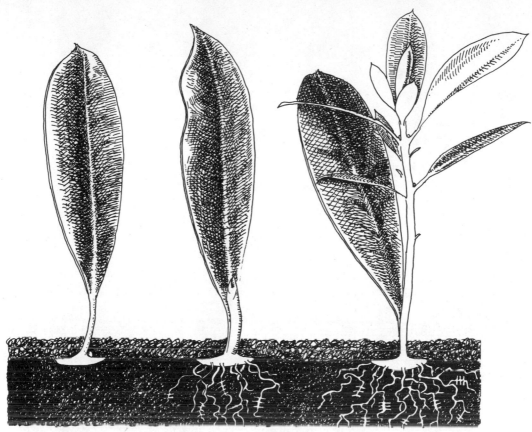

A leaf bud rooting of Rhododendron. Note that the plant actually grows from the small bud between the leaf and branch. The lighter layer of medium above the bud is sand. It holds the leaves vertical but allows air to get to the bud.

both seem to work fairly well. They are taken in July, usually rooted and growing by late September and I harden them by cutting down on their water supply and gradually cooling them for the winter. I transplant in the spring.

Leaf-bud rootings are sensitive and not terribly reliable. A couple of my bushes simply won't do it for me. But I keep on trying because the results are so pleasant.

Root Cuttings

To my mind, root cuttings are quite different from above-ground cuttings for one very significant reason: they are so reliable that even I rarely botch the process. The only shame of it is that more plants can't be propagated in this way. Root cuttings require considerably less care than do any form of stem cuttings and can be grown out-of-doors with almost no special equipment.

Collecting roots, of course, is more difficult than the convenient process of swiping a twig as you walk by a bush. A certain amount of dirt has to be moved and then replaced. But the task isn't as tiresome as you would think and it doesn't begin to approach the

work of a transplanting. I think that my experience with a neighbor's holly might help to explain how to go about it.

I've this neighbor with a holly that is at least eight feet tall. It is a magnificent specimen, with dark, extremely shiny leaves. I wanted it. I knew in advance that he wouldn't give it to me, so I asked if I might take some cuttings from its roots. It took quite a while to convince him that I wasn't mad and that clipping a few of the roots wouldn't be disasterous to the health of his prize. Finally, though, I managed.

I dug three holes six inches in diameter about two feet away from the base of the shrub. I didn't have to go very deep before I ran into a substantial root about a half inch in diameter in each of the holes. After groping around a bit, I cut one piece of flexible root that was about 1/2 inch thick and one piece that was only 1/4 inch thick. Both pieces were three inches long and had several small hair roots. By this time I was tired and my host was losing his confidence in me, so I refilled the holes and made off with the roots.

I should note that these roots were cut in February. Late winter is probably the best time to take such cuttings since the roots are then loaded with reserve nutrition for spring. However, you can as easily take cuttings in the late fall or early winter, so long as you are sure that the plant is dormant.

I filled a pot halfway with a very sandy medium, placed the two roots on the sand and covered them with about a half-inch of sand and peat moss mixed. I covered the mixture with about a half-foot of dried hay and then stood the pot on the porch to wait for spring. The insulating cover served to hold moisture in the soil and so, though I checked with my finger several times, I never had to rewater the roots.

When the temperature rose to 50°, I uncovered the pot, gave it a little water for good measure and waited. As spring progressed, one root took (the smaller one) and put out a fine shoot. That's all there was to it.

As a general rule, woody plants require root cuttings of about a quarter-inch in diameter. Herbaceous plants are generally dug up altogether and divided. These can set up independent operations from roots as fine as one-eighth inch thick. Roots should be from three to five inches long.

There are two kinds of root cuttings, as there seem to be at least two kinds of almost everything. And in root cuttings, as in almost everything, one kind is preferable to the other. I'm often frustrated by those absolutely irrefutable instances of one thing being better than another. By some pugilistic tendency of mind I am inclined to try and argue the benefits of the worst and attack the superior. In some quarters this is referred to as the defense of the underdog, in others, stupid. All too often, though, the reasons for preferring one thing over another are ill-founded or don't relate to what I want.

I have switched paragraphs because I was confusing myself. Switching paragraphs is like clearing my throat.

Now then, there are two kinds of root cuttings, one that is easy to root and one that is more difficult, more challenging and, therefore, more pleasant to succeed with. The more difficult sort is simply a piece of root. It can be found almost anywhere in the rooting system. The easier variety is said to be able to 'see,' that is it has an 'eye' or bud on the root. Such roots are usually found at the base of the plant. They are naturally in the process of putting a shoot up. Many plants that can't be propagated by root cuttings thrive if the root has an eye. (I secretly think of such cuttings as a form of division, not root propagation. And as division (discussed later) is easier than root propagation, I pooh-pooh the whole business. It is, however, only fair to say that when I have failed with a couple of roots, I start looking for one with an eye.).

The Third Kind of Root

There is a third kind of root that I forgot about and am even now a little embarrassed to mention. It is that kind which comes from a plant that has been grafted. There's some information about such graftings later on in the book but, for now, suffice it to say that the top and roots of two different plants are stuck together and grow in such a grafting. This technique is used because the roots can influence the top growth in a number of ways, usually to remain in a dwarfed form. If what you want is what you see growing above ground, you won't get it by propagating one of the roots. You'll get something else entirely. For instance, peach may be growing on quince rootstock. Kind of a shocker to get quince after all that trouble.

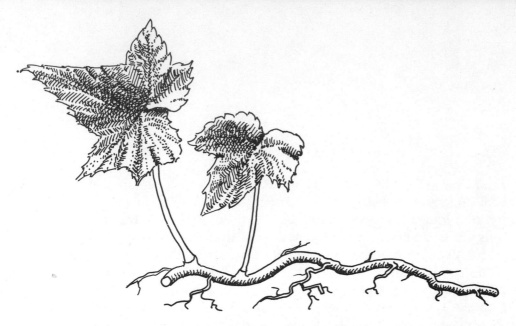

Though I've not been too involved with root cuttings, I have read or heard about success with St.-Johns-Wort, Wisteria, Bittersweet and Mimosa.

Herbaceous plants that work include Bleeding Heart, Anemone, Poppy and Phlox. The later is almost foolproof when propagated in this way.

This is as good a place as any to point out that this book is not filled with lists of plants and their propagating methods. That's so for several reasons. First, it would discourage you from trying things that aren't supposed to work. Second, it would require a great deal of selection in making the list because a thorough one would be miles long. And, finally, propagating a plant is only a part of growing it. You should have some knowledge of many aspects of the things you grow. And that is definitely too big a deal for this book. I strongly suggest you sink the fifteen or twenty or even twenty-five dollars required to buy a giant, hardbound, super-duper encyclopedia of plants. There are several available. Check to make sure that the one you are buying has a subsection under each plant type that gives you propagating methods suitable for that plant. Then, before you venture into the variety, you'll know which methods are suggested by those who do it for a living.

The Transplanting

Regardless of the method of cuttings that you use, whether you are using above-the-ground growth or root cuttings, sooner or later you will have to transplant your new plants. With every kind of rootings, this is a sensitive project and should be treated with considerable respect. Your new roots are very fragile, small and not exactly extensive.

One bit of introductory advice should be dropped in here. As soon as your cutting has established a reasonable number of roots, transplant it. Waiting only causes trouble, not only for the health of the cutting but also for the cutter. With time, cuttings put out enormous amounts of root. And, as they do, they become confused and tangled with other roots from other cuttings. It's bad enough gingerly extracting a fragile cutting when it is only wrapped around perlite. Getting it free of other roots may force you to the most difficult of steps: actually cutting the roots that were so hard won.

A newly-rooted cutting is considerably more fragile than a seedling. The connective tissues binding stem to roots are very weak and the number of roots may be limited. This tenderness is one of the major reasons for the extensive use of perlite and vermiculite instead of peat moss and soil in rooting mediums. The former let go more easily. All you need do, in either case, is dig gently around the plant with a small stick and lift it out. Note that I did not say, nor meant to imply, you should take firm hold of the above-ground cutting and pull. Doing so will damage the thing.

I must now discuss a matter of relative unimportance. I am loathe to do so since it is late at night and I am tired. But I have to. It's my duty or something. Anyway, having extracted your rooted cutting, you have a root ball with some rooting medium stuck to it. You may also find that your roots are all on one side of the cutting. These two problems lead some growers to absurd lengths and arouse some heated discussion.

Some think that the medium ought to be left where it is and the cutting should be planted immediately. The theory here is that removing the medium from close contact with the roots disrupts the contact between root and water.

Some think that the distribution of roots around the stem is important and ought to be symmetrical. Members of this school of thought invariably immerse roots in a saucer of water to remove any remnants of medium and then arrange the root pattern so that it surrounds the base of the stem. Occasionally, of course, all of this orderliness is lost once the roots are pulled from the water. They tangle and mat. Confused by this maze of unkempt roots, some people fill a small pot with water, immerse the roots in it and then fill the pot with soil, thus forcing the water out and potting the cutting all at once. The roots never leave the water. They are

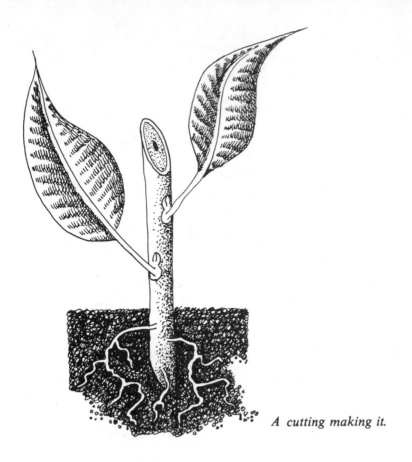

A cutting making it.

beautifully distributed in the soil. And they stay wet. I think that this is a prime example of paranoid overkill. And I refuse to be put down by the implications of such fanatics that I don't love my cuttings as much as they do. I rebut as follows.

Pity the poor cutting that has struggled to set roots in any medium. Its small roots are in hard won, direct contact with the medium and its water. Leave them that way and plant the whole ball directly into the soil. The small amount of nutritionally useless perlite that is left at the base of the plant will soon be overgrown anyway. And my way is easier.

Oh. One other note. And this one is important. Don't pack the soil down after you have potted your new plant. I've already gone through the need for air around a root system. However, it's just as important to a growing plant as to a rooting cutting. And you should take a tip from the Japanese and use only dry soil in a granular condition for potting. This leaves air space. After the potting is completed you can water thoroughly. In fact, in order to keep the constant watering from packing and settling soil in pots, I usually water from below, setting the pot in a deep dish of water for several hours. This allows water to soak upwards, filling the pot without removing air pockets.

This drawing started out to be an illustration of watering from below. It still is. As you can see there's about an inch of water around the pot in the saucer. But I confess to having become much more interested in the leaves of my Peperomia.

Rooting Containers

There are almost as many containers which are suitable for rooting cuttings as there are plants to be grown. A great deal, of course, depends on the time, energy and money you'd like to sink into them and also on the number of cuttings you intend to root. But, regardless of the scope of your ambitions, there is a simple way of building the equipment you need by yourself.

What follows is a roughly progressive overview of different containers. It begins with the simplest of them and moves to more elaborate rigs. Pick up anywhere along the line and work your way as your fanaticism develops.

Polyethylene

Before the mass distribution of polyethylene plastic in America, the propagation of many cuttings was the exclusive province of those with greenhouses. No other feasible way was available for admitting controlled amounts of sunlight and air into an environment that was kept very moist. Plastic, however, changed all that. It is the curious property of this stuff to allow light and air to pass while still holding water. This makes it possible to produce mini-greenhouses of wood and plastic without great expense or space. Plastics also make it possible for you to largely ignore all kinds of rootings for long periods of time. Where once the level of moisture had to be constantly maintained with care, it can now be set and virtually forgotten since it won't change. The water you apply is permanently captured by the plastic.

This water-retention quality of plastic will come up repeatedly in discussions of the containers that are to follow. But there is one point that I should make at the outset. Where the rooting mediums I have suggested up to this point have been designed both to maintain high levels of water and to allow drainage and air, more concern must be shown for drainage when plastic is used. It is such a thorough sealant that too much water in the rooting medium remains too much water. That is, it is held in the medium and never gets a chance to dry out. So, mix your mediums with a little extra sand and a little less peat when plastics are to be used. And be more careful about watering the medium at the beginning. Be sure that it is moist and not wet when you start.

Small, Simple Containers

The oldest small scale hothouse that I know of was introduced to me in the second grade. That lovely old lady gave us each seeds, pots, dirt and a glass jar. This technique works well with small numbers of cuttings. It's compact, versatile, cheap and proven by decades of elementary school classes for whom it has worked perfectly.

A glass jar, capping a cutting, holds moisture around its leaves.

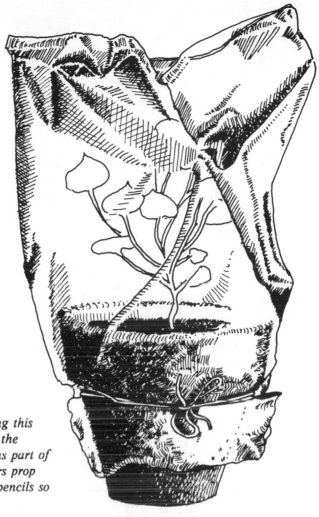

Holding moisture around a cutting this way has been common ever since the sandwich bag became a ubiquitous part of the American home. Some growers prop the bag up over the cutting with pencils so that the plastic doesn't droop.

An adaptation of the glass jar trick has been commonly used since plastic came on the scene. It involves the use of a sandwich bag tied over a pot in one way or another.

Both of these methods serve two purposes. Both cover a certain amount of soil and protect it from losing water to the air, thereby keeping it wet longer. And both create a mini-atmosphere inside the hoods of these containers so that the air around the leaves of the cuttings remains loaded with moisture. This cuts the rate of evaporation from the leaves and allows them to survive longer. It is this moist atmosphere around the cuttings that is most important and that has made it possible to root such plants as Azalea, Yew, Holly and Rhododendron where it would be impossible without a greenhouse.

Another simple method of providing a constant and long-term supply of water for cuttings was introduced to me by the Brooklyn

Botanical Garden in one of their fine special publications. (These are only $1.50 each and worth a lot more.) The method involves the quick production of containers entirely out of plastic. The most direct method is to tie a wad of medium around a cutting. The medium should be moist and tied firmly and will then need no additional water for weeks.

A more unsuspected method is to gather such wrap-ups in a kind of roll-your-own-pot procedure. The advantage here is in keeping the cuttings both thoroughly separated and constantly moist.

Pots That Disappear

Most mail-order nurseries sell some kinds of 'pots' that are transplantable. That is, roots can grow through the walls of these pots and so transplanting, per se, isn't really necessary. You start a

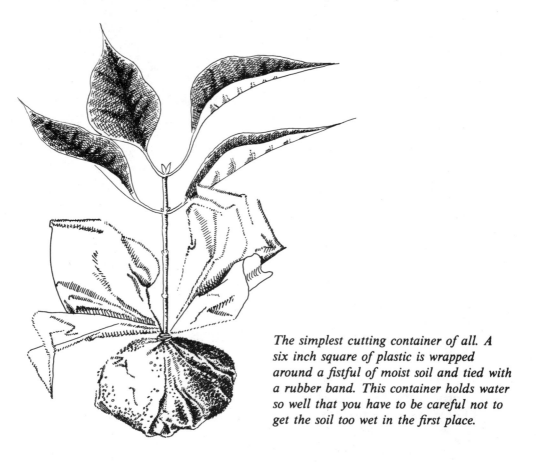

The simplest cutting container of all. A six inch square of plastic is wrapped around a fistful of moist soil and tied with a rubber band. This container holds water so well that you have to be careful not to get the soil too wet in the first place.

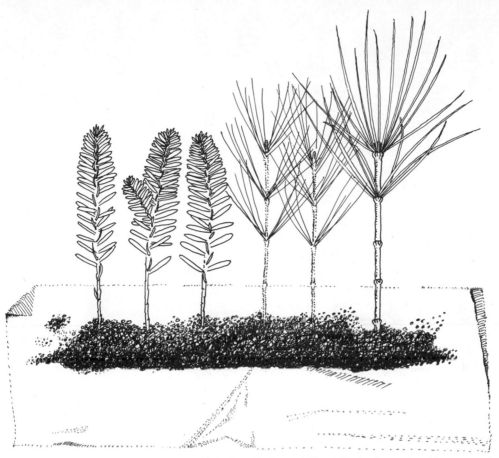

This is a refinement of the simple, single cutting wrap-up. Several cuttings are lined up on a sheet of plastic. Their ends are then covered with medium.

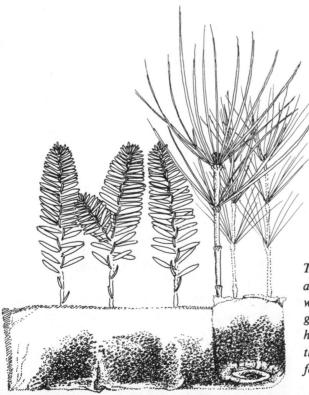

The plastic is then folded over and rolled. Tie the whole thing with string and you've got a container that both holds water and neatly separates the roots of each cutting for you.

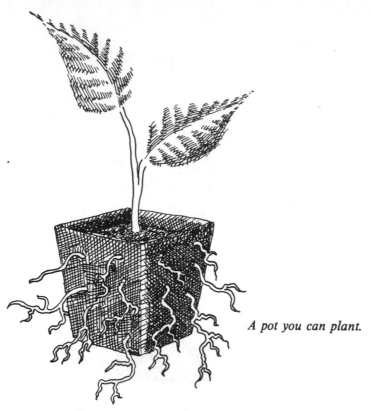

A pot you can plant.

seed or cutting in the pot, treating it as though it were any other medium and then plant the whole works once the roots have set or the leaves appeared from seed.

Some of these cubes are extremely small, only one-half inch on each side. Others are larger and more suited to cuttings. There's only one caution that I should offer here. Some of the more elaborate of these things are compressed peat moss in an expandable plastic sheeting. They are easy to store, come to full size when watered and the plastic keeps them wet for a long time. However, before planting them in a larger container, be sure that you remove the plastic. Roots will not grow through it.

These pots are especially ideal for growing plants for gifts. If you give someone a rooted anything in one of these and they plant and water it, the thing will probably survive. Even the clumsiest of your friends won't destroy your work while transplanting since there's almost no transplanting involved, only the burying of a pot that disappears.

The Forsyth Cutting Pot

This pot is an ingenious solution to the problem of constant water supply. But I think that it is no longer necessary in light of the wide use of plastic. However, it's so clever that I thought I should pass it along to you in case you'd like to try it.

A Forsyth Pot is an azalea pot (one that is two-thirds as wide as it is high) that has a smaller pot set inside it. The outer ring of the

74

azalea pot is filled with rooting medium. The drainage hole in the inner pot is sealed with putty or chewing gum and filled with water. The porous walls of the inner pot allow water to pass slowly into the rooting medium to keep it moist for a long time. A Forsyth pot would almost certainly overwater cuttings, however, if it were covered with plastic.

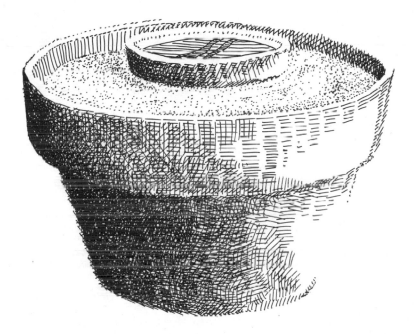

The "Forsyth" cutting pot. A small pot is placed inside a large one and the hole of the smaller pot is plugged. Water, added to the small pot, seeps through its walls gradually watering the soil in the large pot. Clever, huh?

Mini Greenhouses

Much of the seed germination that takes place inside giant nurseries and greenhouses is conducted in flats. Flats are shallow wooden boxes about three or four inches deep and containing some sort of drainage holes. Basically, a seed flat looks like a wooden carton similar to a case of Coke. But without the checkerboard of crosspieces. I know that that's what they look like because that's

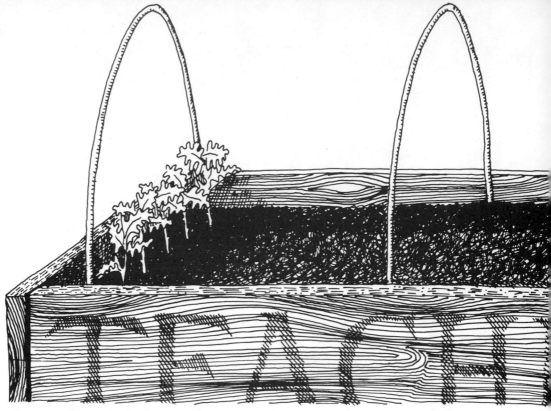

A cutting flat with coat hanger hoops over it. These support a plastic canopy that holds moisture around the cuttings.

what mine are made of. Anyway; these flats are ideal for rooting almost anything. They aren't heavy and they have a great deal of surface area for the rootings.

For years, these flats were enclosed by a pane of glass set on top of the flat. Dowels or some other form of riser were used to allow a small airspace. The seeds germinating inside were kept moist and warm. But there wasn't room under the glass for cuttings. So most cuttings have been propagated in cold frames or in large open greenhouses, the entirety of which are kept moist.

Plastic changed all that, too. By simply bending a few metal coat hangers over a flat and then stretching freezer wrap over the coat hangers, you simulate the perfect greenhouse. There is room inside for cuttings and the atmosphere and soil stay moist for long periods. And the flat is portable. In the case of rooting problems like evergreens, which require some temperature control in winter, you can move the flat when the weather is no longer warm enough for the cuttings.

The polyethylene-covered flat may be rightly said to have ushered in the new age of homebound Johnny Appleseeds. Cuttings and seeds can be propagated in it with tremendous control and in a short time. I'm crazy about mine.

If you are a little more elaborate in your tastes, have more money than I or happen to have killed all your tropical fish, you can try an aquarium or almost any kind of larger plastic container instead of a Coke carton. The aquarium is especially attractive since its glass sides not only admit light but also let you watch what's going on. Some people find watching the roots grow not only fun but helpful in knowing when to transplant. I always think of ant farms when I see roots growing under glass. And there's something in me that feels the lack of privacy and decorum to it is indecent. I also hear and often use the argument that roots dislike light and grow better in the dark. Anyway, as a matter of propriety I would appreciate it if all you aquarium owners would either line the bottoms of your glass-walled planters or keep your cuttings in the middle. Thank you.

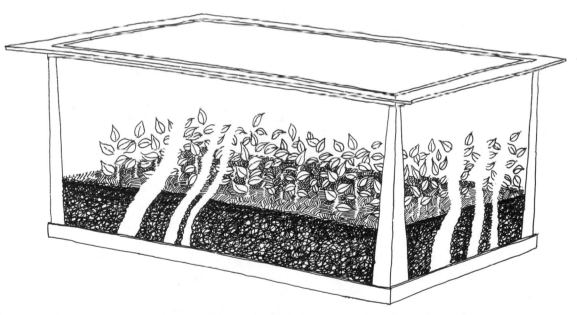

An aquarium with a plate of glass or sheet of plastic over it makes a fine indoor cutting flat.

Cold Frames

Owning a cold frame rates right up there with maintaining a compost pile. It's more than a possession, it's a status. It's more than a status, it's a way of playing on a grand scale that can hardly be equaled.

A cold frame is usually a three foot by six foot box set in the ground and covered by glass or plastic. They are usually made out of 2 × 10's or 2 × 12's of redwood and are often buried several inches into the ground. A cold frame should be built so that it gets full sun. If, during rooting or germination you need to limit the sun, you can do so in a number of ways.

Among the favorite coverings for cold frames is discarded windows. Dumps and the sites of renovations sometimes have them either for the carrying or for cheap sale. It seems to depend on the foreman involved. But you may have a hard time finding one. If so, you can resort to an equally effective substitute of that rippled plastic that is sold in lumber yards and hardware stores. I've done just that.

In order to fully equip your cold frame, you should install some sort of awning facilities for laying cheesecloth over cuttings in the summer. Too much sun on new cuttings dries them out and so you should shade them. An alternative to cheesecloth shade is the age-old use of lathing.

A lathe is a screen of wooden slats that shades plants and cuttings without blocking all sun. The slats are usually 1/4 × 1 inch stock and are suspended running north and south on a frame above the plants. As the sun moves east to west, it crosses the lathing and falls on the plants for short periods of time all day. By adjusting the spacing of the slats, you can very accurately adjust the amount of light falling on your plants and even vary how much light falls on those in one part of your cold frame. Not given to such fine tuning, I simply add another layer of cheesecloth over cuttings that are getting too much sun.

Using a cold frame is a delight in any number of ways. First, it is a large outdoor facility that can accommodate tons of either cuttings or seeds, or both. You don't have to worry about dirt and water getting all over the place. More important is its versatility in terms of the environment you can offer your plants. When cuttings are first placed in a cold frame, you water them and then close the transparent or semi-transparent cover tightly in order to hold water in. At the same time, you should shade the frame somewhat. As rooting occurs and whatever it is you are growing becomes more hardy, you gradually increase the amount of light and inure your plants to the hardships of the world at large by opening the frame slightly. It is in this area of admitting more air that hinged windows prove helpful. They let you prop the covering at any height and slowly increase the air circulation around your plants. Doing so not only hardens your plants but also reduces the likelihood of damping off.

The Ultimate Cold Frame

The ultimate cold frame isn't cold. Hence the name, hotbed. I've often wondered whether a hotbed is more a greenhouse than cold frame and have never managed to answer the question satisfactorily. But, on balance, I think that the relatively low cost of providing your cold frame with artificial heat keeps this from the truly costly world of the greenhouse.

Heat is supplied, generally, by means of insulated cables buried in the sand at the bottom of the frame. These cables are equipped with a thermostat and so allow you to carefully control what goes on inside.

Some people use light bulbs in place of thermostatically-controlled cables. The bulbs, however, are hard to control and are best used in a cold frame only to avoid freezing temperatures, not to start seedlings. They are cheaper but more difficult to use.

Which reminds me of a short, concluding observation on the cold frame. They have a use that is unrelated to the pirating of plants. In fact, I'm not sure which I value more highly, the frame's versatility in propagation or as a protective enclosure for potted outdoor plants in the winter. I drop the pots into my frame and surround them with sand. The frame holds ground heat for a long time and warms quickly in the sun. If the weather gets really ugly, I throw a bedraggled quilt over the whole thing until the cold lets up. Since the same above-freezing temperatures are required for my potted plants and for the rooting of winter cuttings, I succeed on both counts. My Pennsylvania residence and a thick quilt make it a very rare night when the use of a 30 watt bulb is required to keep hard cold from the frame.

Layering

Layering is probably the oldest asexual propagating method. It is the technique of rooting a part of a plant without disconnecting it from the main plant. It is a kind of cutting, in a way, but with a conservative wrinkle: some of the sustaining support of the main plant is preserved, though often reduced, while roots are being encouraged.

Layering is both pleasant and versatile for a number of reasons. The most important one to me is its ease. Since the layered part is left attached to the main branch, it becomes much more difficult to kill. But there are ramifications to this insurance. The most obvious is that some of the desperation is taken out of the process and the layered part is in no way forced by the almost immediate threat of death to produce roots. Injuring the branch in question will stimulate root production and the advent of plastics and rooting hormones helps, but layering usually takes quite a lot longer than rooting cuttings.

But the point is not so much that layering takes longer than rooting cuttings. Rather, you layer something because it won't root from cuttings since it is naturally so slow that it would die. Layering, then, is used on those parts of plants that are difficult or impossible to root from cuttings. Before the widespread use of polyethylene and mist propagation a great many plants were reproduced this way. But now, with more modern facilities and methods helping cuttings to stay alive longer and hormones helping them to root faster, layering has gone out of fashion. Since almost anything can now be rooted from cuttings in far greater numbers and with more convenience than with layering, few nurseries bother with the slower method anymore.

But the amateur may have good reason for layering. As I said, it's easier and less likely to fail than growing cuttings. And the flaw in layering that discourages large growers, that it is difficult to produce huge numbers of new plants this way, doesn't relate to you and me. And the technique will probably always retain its unique ability to propagate large pieces of plants that could not be rooted on their own. With patience and care, branches as large as your wrist can be rooted this way.

But all those are the considerations of reasonable men. Certainly I could expand upon the matters of ease and reliability. I could continue to tell you about how you need to produce only a few and not hundreds of new plants and would probably rather they were large than small. I could go on with good, sound reasons for the amateur's interest in layering almost forever. Honest, I could.

But the trick is in the fun, not in the benefits of any one method over another under well-considered circumstances. And let me tell you, this is fun.

The Chinese, and later the Japanese, practiced the art of marcottage, or air layering, thousands of years ago. Their technique was relatively simple and hasn't changed much since. Modern materials and methods have made air layering much simpler than it was then but the approach is the same. The Chinese gardener had to be incredibly committed to whatever it was he wanted to root. His method was painstaking and slow and required almost constant care.

A branch was wounded at the point where roots were expected to grow. Moss, soil and sand were matted around the wound in a large ball and tied in place. Then, several times a day, each time checking the moisture level in the ball, it was watered. Several times a day for a couple of years. That was the method. But you have to screw up your eyes and think hard to imagine the effort that went into such a rooting. There are very few instances that I can think of where that sort of patience is practiced anymore. Things happen quicker, are expected to, and they invariably happen hundreds and thousands at a time. The idea of working hard to create one lousy plant is defunct.

Except in books like this one and backyards like mine. The unreasonable and indefensible occurs there with stunning regularity. For instance, I'm the sort of fool who layers something that I could root by cutting. Not only that, but I'll layer a small twig, nullifying the advantage of size. And, on occasion, I'll avoid the use of plastic and hormone just to see if I can do it.

I think that I mentioned before that I have a small but thriving split leaf maple that I rooted. My grandfather grew the original about fifty years ago from a seedling. My father now owns it. And I air layered another for my garden. I don't know why I went to all the trouble exactly. I could have taken a couple of dozen cuttings and rooted them under plastic. But then eight or ten would have taken and all I wanted was one.

There's a naturalness and comic pleasure to layering that I swear rivals the seed. Natural because fallen and drooping trees and shrubs often layer themselves. In the wild, Rhododendrons do it all the time. But more important, I think, is the comedy of layering. Both slapstick and classical. Certainly there's something funny about a wad of earth hung on a tree or a low branch dipped into the ground and then staked next to the main plant. I'm reminded of Mutt and Jeff by the tall and tiny duo. And then there's the classic comedy of rebirth and growth. Of things happening over again, of going on and being okay, and I like being part of that. I guess you can understand that my attitude is untenable for those who have to make a living at propagation. But, as I said before, I'm not so much a propagator as a plant pirate, stealing from the world what it would give up anyway and not so much for the stolen thing as for the fun of plundering it in the first place.

Basic Layering

The simplest form of layering (often referred to as 'simple') involves bending over a low-hanging branch until it can be buried. It's a straightforward method often used on Rhododendrons, Yews and Azaleas. Generally, layering is begun in the spring before the buds begin to open. It's at this time that the most substantial energies of the plant are about to be directed towards growth and so it has the resources available for root development. As in cuttings, the younger the shoot, the more it is apt to root. With cuttings, of course, still-maturing growth is used. In layering this isn't possible (unless you want to begin the layer in the fall), so year old branches are used.

Step number one is predictable but often overlooked: choose a very healthy branch that can be bent easily to the ground. Don't pick an old or overgrown branch. They aren't nearly so vigorous.

Then add peat moss or sphagnum and some sand to the soil you

Ground layering involves burying a healthy branch so that it's submerged part will grow roots.

intend to use in burying the layer. Show this dirt all the respect and concern you would the rooting medium you use for cuttings.

There are two approaches to the wounding of a layered branch. Both apply to all layering. The oldest form is the removal of a band of bark around the limb. This incision should be made only deep enough to remove the bark and *injure*, not mutilate, the cambium layer just beneath it. The second method is to make a slanting cut into the branch about half way through it. Then a clean pebble or stick is wedged in this opening to hold it open so it won't heal instead of rooting.

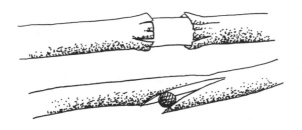

The exposed inner surfaces of the branch are coated with rooting hormone. You can do this with your finger but a small paint brush works better.

The branch is then buried about two inches in the soil at the point where the cut has been made. Some gardeners prefer to build a mound over the branch rather than bury it. I can't see any difference other than that burying it seems wetter. The choice, then, depends on your climate. As in the rooting of cuttings, too much water is as bad as too little. In burying the branch, be sure that the tip is left above ground.

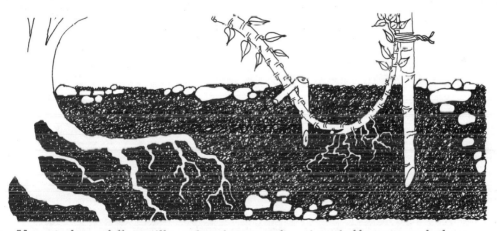

If you look carefully you'll see that there is a slice about half way through the buried branch and a pebble holding this slice open. It's in and around this slice that you put rooting hormone.

You must then hold the limb down one way or another. I use hooks cut from trees but others use bricks and large stones put on top of the soil.

If you layer in the spring, you should wait until the next spring to dig and remove the rooted piece. If the job was done in the fall, wait a year and a half.

Show the same care in digging your plant up that you would show a fragile new rooting of any kind. Be especially concerned if the branch is a large one because it will need all the roots it has. Cut the branch just below the roots and coat the cut with a fungicide. Then plant it as you would any seedling.

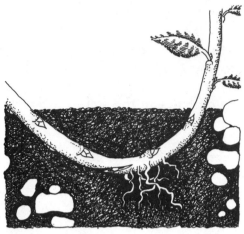

You can see the hoped-for roots and slice clearly here.

Tip Layering

Tip layering is very much like simple layering. The major distinction is that the tip of a shoot is buried at the beginning of the growing season. As this bud grows quickly, it usually breaks above ground and sets roots by the end of the growing season. You can then feel confident about removing it once dormancy sets in and very confident if you wait until the following spring to dig.

Tip layering. Rather than bury a branch so that it goes into and then out of the ground, an active terminal bud is buried. When it grows it will set roots.

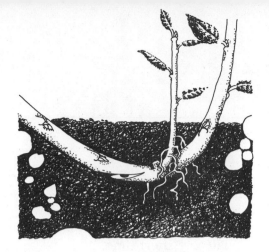

This refinement involves scarring the top side of the buried branch so that it will sucker. Suckers grow roots quickly and can be removed later, leaving their roots to feed the main branch.

Elaborations

There are a few refinements that have been made in simple layering that may help you if you are either in need of several plants or have a hard time getting yours to root.

First, you can induce suckers (fast-growing shoots) in a simple layer by injuring the top side of the buried branch. Often this injury creates a sucker that grows both leafy and root portions quickly. The shoot and leaves are allowed to grow awhile and then are removed, the roots being left in place to feed the prime portion of the layer.

Further refining this technique, you can make several ruptures below ground and, once rooted, separate and grow the suckers themselves.

Finally, you can bury your branch porpoise-fashion, leaving exposed side branches whenever possible. Make cuts and treat with hormone as in simple layering and you will end up with several plants.

This is a neat and challenging variation that you can try if a low branch has suitable side shoots.

Mound Layering

This method of layering was developed for commercial use in Europe. It produces a relatively large number of progeny in a relatively short time.

Mounding takes advantage of the readiness of new growth to strike roots. You simply cut a many-shooted plant back almost to ground level and allow new, fast-growing shoots to appear. Since the method was created for the sake of quantity, it is usually practiced on crowned plants that habitually produce many shoots when pruned in this way.

Sometimes, small incisions are made in these shoots and these cuts are coated with hormone. Sometimes not.

The new shoots are then half-buried in soil, forming a mound over the old crown. Rooting occurs in the shoots and they are separated a year later.

Mound layering. The main trunk is cut just above the ground, forcing suckers. These are buried, grow roots and can later be removed separately.

Removed from the ground, a layer should look something like this

Air Layering

This is the most difficult form of layering. It involves considerable care and a rather precise sense of the meaning of the word 'moist.'

The major reason for the failure of air layers before the widespread use of plastic was the drying out of the root ball. Since the use of plastic, the biggest problem has been the too thorough retention of water. In order both to root and not rot an air layer, you must keep a constant but not too abundant supply of water against the shoot or branch. Since you're tying that water in a confined space of sphagnum and plastic, no water can escape. If you put too much in or allow any to be added, you will rot the branch.

I use sphagnum exclusively in air layers. It holds water well and inhibits the growth of fungi. But I am very careful to soak and then wring it out before applying to the wound of the branch. Also, don't wrap the sphagnum itself too tightly. Allow plenty of airspace.

Wrap polyethylene around the wad of sphagnum and seal each end of it with rubber bands or string. Be very careful to cover all parts of the sphagnum and of the wound. They dry quickly otherwise.

All other aspects of air layering are exactly the same as those of simple layering. The wound, hormone, removal and planting techniques work well for both.

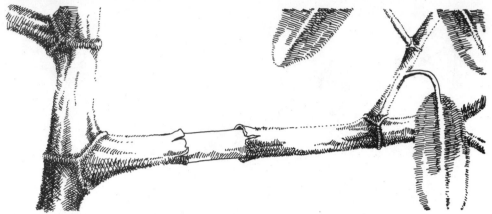

The ancient art of air layering, nobly illustrated and cleverly adapted to the modern technique of polyethylene moisture retention. In this first picture the bark of the branch has been removed in a band about an inch wide. Rooting hormone (unknown to the ancients) is liberally applied to the wound.

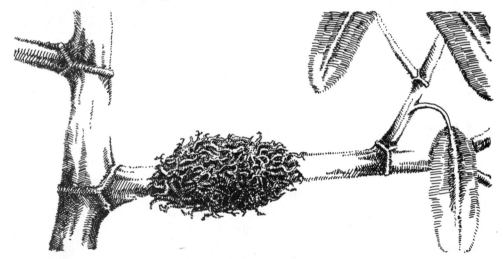

Moist sphagnum moss is wrapped around the wound.

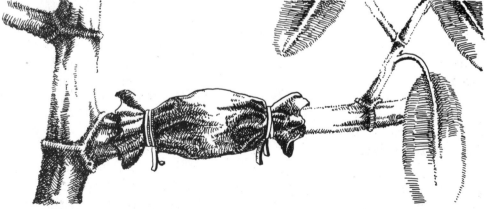

And plastic is tied around the moss. I use cut rubber bands for this. After an interminable wait roots may or may not appear under the plastic, fill the sphagnum and so signal the time for transplanting.

Planting a Layered Branch

Other than failures due to too much water, the prime cause of lost layerings is impatience in planting and hardening the newly-won tree. The usually extensive top growth of a recently cut layer is supported by a fragile and small root system. In order to make this as healthy a situation as possible, you should wait as long as you can before separating it from the main plant. If you use plastic, this means until you can see that the root ball is loaded with roots.

After separating the layer, you should plant it with the care of any newly-rooted plant. And then you should keep it out of direct sunlight and make certain that it is moist for about a month. Give it plenty of time to become accustomed to its autonomy before beginning to increase gradually the amount of sun it gets.

Naturally Layering Plants

There are plants that have developed a marked inclination for layering themselves. Nature has provided them with branches or stems that grow out and then down and that grow new plants at their ends. These constantly-spreading plants are, in essence, a further development of the enthusiastic variety of viviparous leaves discussed in the cuttings chapter. Such layering plants produce stems and branches that go by several names. Some are called offsets, some runners and others stolons.

A Raspberry stolon.

An offset is a shoot that grows from a plant and produces roots quickly and easily when it bends and touches the ground.

A runner is a very long offset that often produces marked plantlets containing both leaves and roots. The Spider Plant (Chlorophytum elatum) and the Strawberry Begonia (Saxifraga sarmentosa) are examples of extremely prolific runner plants.

A stolon is essentially a runner. However, the distinction between them is that runners usually produce leaves in clumps along their lengths even if they don't root or touch ground. Stolons do not. They have to touch down first, strike roots and then produce foliage.

Such easy-to-layer plants are a joy. If grown indoors, all you have to do is put a pot under the end of any such growth and wait for it to root. Once it has, you just cut it from the main plant. Most root so quickly that they can be treated like very agreeable stem cuttings and removed from the plant before they have rooted. They will almost always survive this treatment.

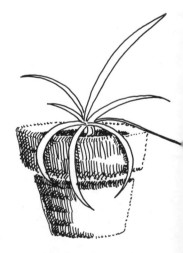

Spider plants are so inviting that they are almost irresistable. They can be separated and rooted without much risk, but there's something to this method that I like.

Grafting and Budding

A graft is the physical union of two pieces from separate plants to form a single individual. The two grow together, healing the gap between them.

Grafting is not a simple form of propagation. It isn't used to produce new plants so much as to produce special types of plants that could not be grown otherwise. It takes a certain amount of skill and a decided knowledge of what you're grafting to what and why.

Grafts are usually made because a variety of plant does not grow true to seed and is extremely difficult either to layer or root from cuttings. If you've ever saved a cherry pit or planted an apple seed, you may have been lucky enough to have it grow. If so, you have almost certainly been unhappy to discover that not only was the tree that resulted singularly unattractive but also produced fruit that tasted terrible. This is the result of the curious ancestry of the tree that produced the fruit in the first place. Many such trees produce seeds with almost random genetic qualities and so equally random seedlings and fruit. In order to maintain a high-quality line of fruit trees, then, cuttings must be made from a successful tree and grafted on established roots.

Apples are grafted or budded to apples, peaches to wild peaches, and some pears to quince. The above-ground portion of the resulting tree is rarely influenced by the roots on which it relies. The rootstock is chosen for its hardiness, its ease of rooting and its compatibility with the above-ground growth (called the scion).

Compatibility is very important here. You can't just stick a piece of some tree on another and expect it to survive. Generally, you should try grafting a tree only to one like it. Apple to apple, peach to peach, etc. However, there are a few exceptions that are especially useful to the amateur and I'll mention them later on.

Just beneath the bark of a tree is a layer of fleshy material called the cambium. Beneath it is the woody section of the tree. It is the cambium layers of the understock (part with roots) and the scion that must grow together. The larger the surface of the cambium layers that are touching, the more likely the graft will succeed. In many cases you'll find that the rootstock is larger than the scion. If so, be sure to slide the scion to one side. If you center it, the cambium layers of the two parts will not be touching.

There are reasons for grafting other than the inability of seeds to grow true to type or the difficulties of rooting cuttings. One that is common among nurseries is the lethargy with which some varieties of plant grow if produced on their own roots. Lilacs, for instance, are slow on their own. So commercial nurseries graft them on Privet. This produces a larger plant more quickly and so is more profitable for the grower. The problem with this sort of graft (as with others as well) is that the rootstock may produce suckers that, of course, are very different from what is wanted. Such shoots have to be watched for and removed. In the case of the Lilac, you can usually plant one deeply and it will set its own roots while surviving and growing on those of the Privet.

There are other influences that rootstocks can exert on a plant. The one most interesting to the gardener is the tendency for some to dwarf the resulting tree. In today's small gardens this is especially useful. And, happily, the fruit from such trees is almost always normal size. I should say, though, that speeding up or dwarfing the growth of the above-ground tree is about the only influence that the rootstock has. The scion retains is genetic makeup. In fact, grafting is used in order to preserve that makeup long beyond the life of a single tree.

Grafting

Grafting and budding are governed by the same rules of compatibility, so the final section of this bit on grafting applies to both. Be sure to refer to it before you try anything.

The varieties of graft depend only on the styles of union between the scion and rootstock. And I think that the pictures and their captions take care of that pretty well. However, there are a few considerations common to all grafts that you should know about.

The most important is one relating to all propagation and so shouldn't come as much of a surprise at this point. A grafting scion is essentially a cutting that is being asked to establish roots via another plant. That's going to take some time, of course, and while it's going on, there is certainly going to be a drain of water from the scion. The most significant area of the scion is the cambium layer at the joint and so it is here that you have to be particularly careful about it drying out.

Most grafts are tightly (maybe snuggly is a better word) secured with an elastic wrap of some kind. Rubber bands work fine. The give of the wrap allows the tree to grow without being choked, but firm contact is maintained so that the union doesn't move while it is

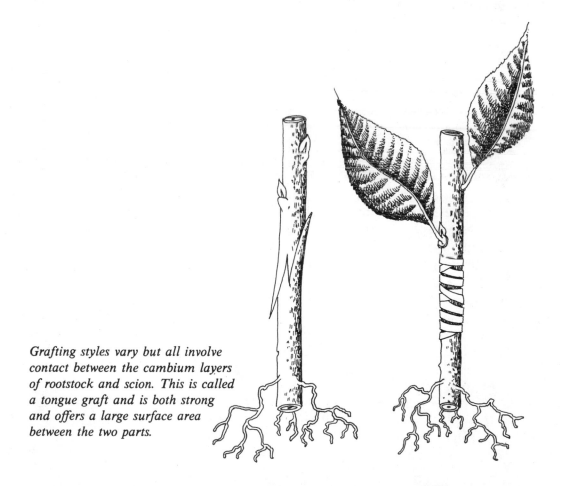

Grafting styles vary but all involve contact between the cambium layers of rootstock and scion. This is called a tongue graft and is both strong and offers a large surface area between the two parts.

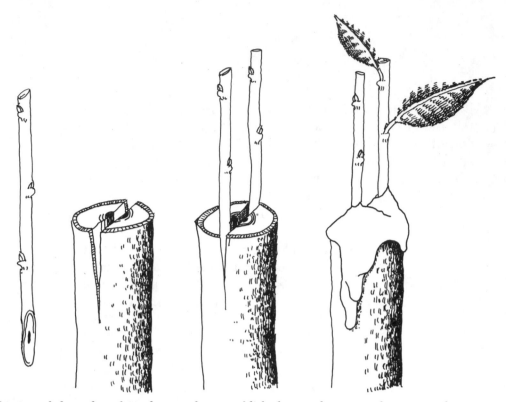

This is a cleft graft and is often used on established trees that are to be converted. Note the wax covering the wound.

healing. And then wax is applied over the meeting place so that water doesn't escape and so that dirt and infection don't get in.

I've a friend who then treats the graft like an air layering, wrapping and sealing it with plastic. He also treats the top of the scion like a cutting, tying a plastic sandwich bag over it until the graft is complete and the threat of moisture loss is over. It's a sensible procedure and seems to work well for him.

Scion grafts (as opposed to bud grafts) are usually made in the winter. They should be kept tied throughout the next growing season or at least until the scion is obviously growing. Ideally, the scion should be dormant and the understock should be just beginning to grow when the union is made. Since this is a little difficult, the advice above concerning grafting in the winter is common. It's more important to give the scion its dormancy than the rootstock its activity. However, some very clever people from somewhere (Dear Sir: My notes don't tell me where I read this idea, so I can't credit you. But, thanks, whoever you are. Peter.) suggested that the scions be cut in February or March and put in the refrigerator until the understocks begin to become active.

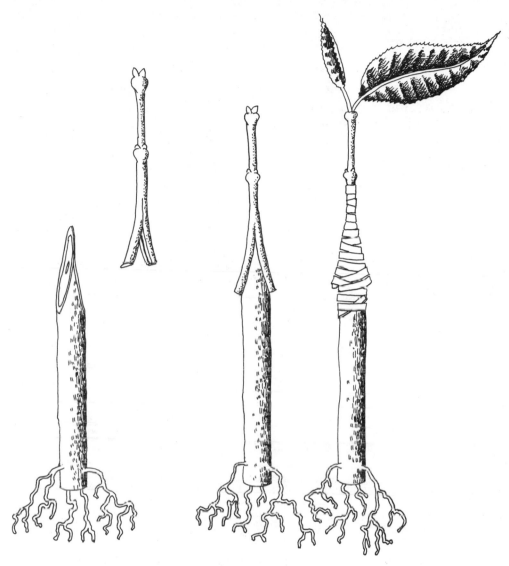

A saddle graft. This style is used when quick growth is expected of the scion. Once that growth is established the plant is buried so that part of the scion is underground. As in mound layering the scion will often then set its own roots.

Budding

Budding is probably the most common commercial form of graftage. It, quite wonderfully, produces all of a fruit-bearing tree from a single bud inserted into the bark of a rooted sapling about the size of a pencil.

Budding is almost always done in the spring. There is much less hassle over the dormancy of the buds since most of them are easily

99

found dormant anyway. You should follow the same advice of tying and waxing buds as other scions.

I hope the pictures explain the process.

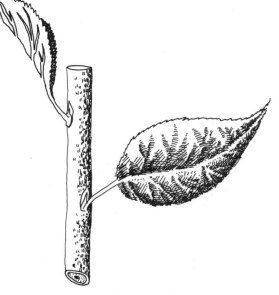

Budding is begun with a branch from the variety you wish to grow above ground.

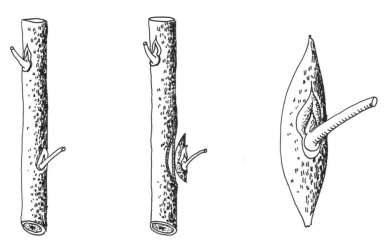

Leaves are removed but an inch-long bit of stem is left as a handle. Then slice through the bark, removing a more or less boat shaped piece of stem, bud and bark.

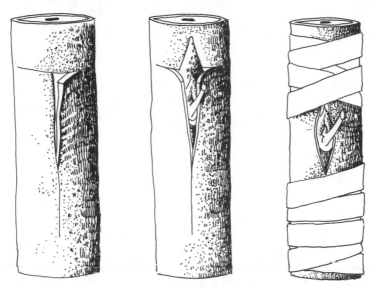

The rootstock is prepared by making a T-shaped cut in the bark. This cut should not go into the cambium layer. The 'T' is opened and the bud inserted. Then the bud is tied with elastic bands so that growth won't scar the bark.

The Shocking Lack of Readily Available Rootstock

Commercial firms that do a considerable amount of grafting buy their understock, rooted, from other companies that do nothing but produce such stuff. But you can't. Rootstock suppliers sell only to the trade, as they say. And you probably won't be able to convince your local nursery to do you a favor and sell you any, either. So you'll have to grow your own from cuttings or seed. That's not as difficult as it might sound and you can get the seed from large mail-order suppliers.

But, occasionally you'll run into a problem. Some years ago, I used to climb around in a huge McIntosh apple tree with a friend from school and hide in the leaves of it, eating apples and sneaking cigarettes. I'm not sure I enjoyed the cigarettes but I loved the tree and its apples. So, when I grew up (?) and didn't have to sneak my cigarettes anymore, I wanted a McIntosh apple tree of my very own. But I wanted a dwarf because I haven't grown up enough yet to have a lot of land. Well, McIntosh apple cuttings aren't hard to come by but the rootstock that dwarfs them is. It's called Malling 9. And it's almost impossible to find a Malling 9 tree anywhere to take cuttings or layerings from. So, being ingenious and stubborn, I finally found an acquaintance of a friend with a penchant for Delicious apples and with a dwarf of the same. He was happy to let me dig a root from his tree and I grafted my Mac directly on the root. I confess to being surprised that it worked. But it did.

If you're interested in dwarfing fruit trees, good luck. I'm told that there are seed importers who specialize in such things. But I am not involved enough in it (and don't know anyone who is) to find out. Sorry. My only suggestion to you if you are interested in the idea is to spend the money to buy a dwarf with a named rootstock and use one of the many propagating methods suitable to develop rootstock from its roots. I think that this would be the easiest, cheapest and most reliable way. Incredible as it may seem after having just paid good money for a grafted dwarf, I would suggest you cut it off below the graft scar. This will force rootstock suckers the next spring that you can work with.

As to other compatible scions and rootstocks, here's a list.

Scion	Rootstock
Apple	Almost any other apple.
Apple (semi-dwarf)	Malling 7
Apple (dwarf)	Malling 9
Apricot	Almost any other apricot
Azalea	*Azalea ponticum*
Cherry	Mazzard Cherry *(P. avium)*
Crab Apple	Almost any other apple.
Dogwood (Cornus)	*C. forida*
Flowering Quince	*Cydonia japonica*
Peach	Grow from almost any peach pit.
Peach (dwarf)	Bessey cherry *(P. besseyi)*
Pear	From seeds of Bartlett or Beurre hardy.
Plum	Cherry plum
Prune	Bessey cherry *(P. besseyi)*
Rose	*R. multiflora*
Yew	*Taxus cuspidata*

Seeds

Among the more peculiar properties of my mind is the tendency to convert relatively sensible and concrete scientific theories into less sensible, far more elusive observations. Working with seeds has prompted just such a Tobeyesque distillation of Darwin's theories of natural selection and evolution.

It seems that Darwin said that changes occur in nature quite by chance and that competition among creatures favors those best suited to survive a particular environment. Darwin observed that as a result of this selection in favor of better versions of old animals, species evolved into new species.

Looked at differently, that means that almost anything can happen, and probably will, until it goes right. For it seems that no matter how unlikely or grotesque are the requirements for change, they pop up anyway. Somewhere in the scheme of things there is a curious tendency in directions as yet unexplored that is frustrated only by failure. In other words, the part of the world that we get to watch seems to say to us that not everything is possible but everything ought to be tried anyway because the most unlikely things can work. And the major conclusion that I draw from this garbled ninth-grade biology is that Nature is trying to encourage pipe dreams by showing us that success is a stubborn and inexplicable creature that occurs in spite of apparent foolishness and certain doom.

I begin this chapter on seeds with that unhorticultural, in fact slightly unreasonable, rambling because I am sitting here with my typewriter thinking about propagation in general and seeds specifically. And I notice that the many different methods of asexual propagation discussed in this book, though practical, ubiquitous and ancient, are really amazing. Nature seems to have developed a remarkable set of survival tactics for her fellows. Looked at one way, it's all simply mundane and stubborn. An adaptive process that has been honed through time and necessity. But, if you allow yourself a bit of whimsy, you can see the same goings on in very pleasant ways. Trees and vines and roots rub together and join, becoming stronger. Bits of trees break off and, by wind or water, travel to new places and grow. And the old lie down and start over, layering in the leaves.

And more amazing, all these nomadic tendencies in plants are only the occasional life boats, the auxiliary systems of their survival. And though quirky and interesting and unusual, they are really nothing compared to the big banana, sexual propagation by seeds.

Seeds are where it's at in nature. They are the primary way that things spread themselves around. Seeds make everything else look marginal, as though Nature developed all those other means of pirating plants as a kind of hobby so that the real work would seem that much more wonderful and basic.

A few examples may help explain my ramblings on the subject of seeds. Consider for the moment the size of the Begonia seed. An ounce contains millions of them. Or consider that one plant is capable of producing literally millions of offspring in a matter of a few seasons. Puts the rabbits to shame. You can freeze seeds, cook 'em, store them for years, soak them, do all sorts of uncomfortable things to them and they, for the most part, hang in there.

With my penchant for admiring the ability to move plants from where they are to where you want them, I notice not only the stunning act of seeds turning into plants but also their means of moving around. The wind blows Dandelion and Milkweed all over. Maples heliocopter around and Catalpas seem to have a purpose to their soaring. Coconuts raft across oceans, Burdock hops freight on the fur of animals, Apples get eaten so that their seeds will travel with the eater. And practically every berry you can imagine gets flown in the belly of a bird at one time or another. Squirrels carry Oak and Walnut seeds around. And there are plants, like Witch Hazel, Boxwood and the Squirting Cucumber that shoot their seeds out by a ripening process that catapults them many feet.

But, before getting into the human use of all this fertility, I should explain something of the basic process of germination. I find, after consulting my dictionary, that to say that seeds are prolific is almost redundant. But I would still like to say that, though it is remarkable you can grow a tree from a small cutting, it is more remarkable still that you can grow one from a seed. I'm sorry I am making such a fool out of myself about this. But I can't help it. There is something grotesquely beautiful about the process that I admire and enjoy. So, here,

An Oversimplified Archetype of Seed Germination

Consider the seed carefully and you have to admit that the child is ugly. I have long felt that no great work of literature could be written without saying as much. It's one of those truths that is always avoided, especially by mothers. But it's true of seeds just as it's true of any other child.

A seed is a developing embryo. It is a bunched up bundle of basic requirements capable of turning into something. Seeds contain a primary root and a primary shoot attached to an original, or "seed leaf" (called cotyledons). These elemental parts are packaged in a coating of one kind or another. On one end of the coating is a small scar where it was attached to the parent. Close to this scar is a hole through which the root will grow when the time is right. Inside the coating is a certain amount of stored nutrients that will be used to produce the enormous amount of energy that is needed for the embryo to develop and exist on its own.

That's about all there is to it. A basic, pale bundle. Around the seed there may be an added coating such as those found in beans or apples. But that's not really part of the seed. It is simply a coating of fertilizer and moisture intended to improve the soil where the seed falls.

Germination

Seeds germinate, or break out of their coating and begin to develop beyond their embryonic status, when they come in contact with the proper environment. Generally, it means that they are moist, warm (about 60 to 65°F) and have a supply of air around them. Some require light, some don't care and others are inhibited by it.

If the folded stem, root and leaf of an ungerminated seed are pathetically small and pale, they are nevertheless enormously powerful. But, for all the energy that they release in germinating and beginning growth, they are still somehow grotesque. At least I think so. The new plant sets a root, flies its shoot and early leaves and then hopes for the best. And I find this tenuous hold on life so beautiful and fragile that I am upset, even angry, almost sickened by its vulnerability. It must have all the right conditions of moisture, warmth and air to make it and it has to hurry. It's going to live the early part of its life on stored resources. It must grow considerably before the first leaves appear and photosynthesis begins. It can take in no foods from the surrounding environment until those leaves are out. A hairy situation at best.

Having set leaves, the root system grows, the body of the plant develops in any number of ways, water is absorbed, photosynthesis occurs and the plant is on its way. However, it is fragile for a long time. It needs the right amount of light and constant water. Too much light will overpower its water supply. Cold will stop it altogether. And just the right kinds and amounts of foods have to be available for growth.

That is the process through which seeds go in order to turn into seedlings. There are any number of variations on the theme, differences in maturing rates, moisture requirements and the like. And you have to know several pages of additional material to make it work right. But that's what happens. And I guess that the thing about it all that most impresses me is, somehow, at the core of the matter. I mean that small things can be helped to grow into big things. That propagation works and that it's almost free. It's like borrowing for the asking the accumulated talents of eons of evolution and adaptability. And that's why I started all this with so much glop on the marvels of plant life. I hope that having done so will help you grow seeds or that it will at least have changed your attitude toward them.

Dormancy

Many seeds germinate as soon as they are ripe if put in the proper environment. Vegetables and annuals are among those with which most people are familiar. Tomato seeds need only be cleaned and dried and they are then ready to be planted. What's more, they can be stored for long periods. Most seeds are germinateable (known by those in the know as viable) even after a year or two in storage. But some plants do not produce seeds which are ripe immediately.

By 'ripe' I mean a number of different phenomena for which there are many explanations. But nobody seems to be very sure what's going on. Generally, we think of a thing as ripe when it can be eaten. More important to this discussion, it seems that a seed should be considered ripe when it falls off of the plant. But it isn't necessarily viable yet. Some seem to continue developing on the ground, requiring any number of internal changes forced by their environments. In order to get these seeds to grow, you have to put them through these changes. They are 'dormant' and will not germinate until they have matured.

This is probably the place for a sweeping remark on the point of seed-growing techniques. In every way possible, your job is to imitate the natural conditions that the seed needs. You are supposed to fake what would ideally go on if the seed were left alone in nature.

This is especially significant when it comes to various kinds of dormancy. In order to survive, seeds are sometimes equipped with apparatus that frustrates human control. This is not the result of perverse effort by Nature to make your life miserable. The special equipment is there to help the seed make it in the wild, where it may fall on hard times. In your seed flat or cold frame, that which would help elsewhere can hurt. So you have to simulate those conditions occurring in nature which make the seed mature and become viable. In some cases, this involves the removal of impermeable coatings or fleshy insulations. In other cases, strange, internal clocks have to be satisfied by artificial means. But it all comes down to doing what nature would do over a longer period of time and with a lower success rate.

Things to do to Seeds

Most of what follows is about what you must do to seeds to get them to germinate. But I would like to state the obvious first so you'll know what to do to seeds in order to store them. Seeds should be clean and dry to prevent rotting. Beyond that, you should keep them from those conditions which cause them to germinate. Obvious? Sure. Because seeds like warmth, moisture, light and air, you store them by putting them in a sealed jar in a cool, dry, dark place. Most seeds will keep for years this way.

Now, about getting them mature so that they germinate. The most difficult hurdle to overcome in maturing dormant seeds is dealing with those that have internal clocks. Some seeds are designed so that they require the pattern of cold temperatures in winter before they are ready to germinate in spring. This is, I think, an effort on the designer's part to keep the seeds from being tricked by a warm fall day. If they were to germinate on such a day, winter would clobber them shortly thereafter. So, they need several months of cold to mature. Simulating winter is called stratification.

Stratification

Woody plants like Flowering Dogwood and Pine require a cold period between the time they are ripe enough to fall from the tree and before they germinate. Some growers refer to this period of necessary cold as 'after ripening,' but the name is not based on any concrete knowledge of what is actually going on inside the seed.

Anyway, such seeds have to be kept cool for from one to four months. They are cleaned, soaked for twenty-four hours or so and packed in moist sawdust, sphagnum, sand or some combination thereof and then refrigerated. The name stratification is derived from arranging layers (strata) of medium and seeds in a flat, usually with about two inches of sawdust between the layers of seeds. This method is still used, but the use of plastic bags is much more common and convenient. You simply spread the seeds through the mixture and tie the bag.

Stratification by the gardener is usually planned so that the seeds never freeze. In nature, of course, many freeze over the winter. And many die as a result. In order to up the percentage of the seeds that are viable, you should keep them at about 40°. You can do this in a cold frame over the winter, if you insulate it against hard freezing temperatures, or you can put your baggie filled with seeds and sawdust in the back of the refrigerator. The latter is usually preferable. The temperature is more constant and seeds are small enough not to take up too much room.

(As I've mentioned somewhere else in this book, I'm not going to give long lists of seeds and their respective needs. I would only be incomplete. Go out and buy an encyclopedia of plants. Buy one with headings under each plant on their proper propagation and follow their directions. It's a much more thorough way of finding out what to do than the scope of this book could offer.)

Double Dormancy

Double dormancy is the even more elaborate need of some plants for variations in temperature over time so that they can become viable. Such plants require a certain period of warm temperatures followed by cold and followed again by warm for germination. If planted outdoors in the fall when they are first ripe, these plants take two seasons to sprout. They need the warmth of the first summer to 'ripen,' the next winter to 'stratify' and then germinate in the spring.

Cotoneaster, Hawthorn and Cranberry are among these plants. Cotoneaster, for instance, requires three or four months of 60 to 75° temperatures and then three or four months of 40° temperatures before it germinates when again put in a 60° environment with warmth, moisture, light and air. You can put such seeds in plastic bags, leave them at room temperature for a couple of months and then refrigerate them. By doing so, you can usually hurry the process enough to plant in May or June.

Other Dormancies

There are two other significant sources of dormancy that delay the germination of a seed. The first is simply a matter of Nature's having done too good a job of protecting the seed in the first place. The coating is so hard that water cannot penetrate to trigger germination. And, in some cases, even if some water does penetrate, the hard coating restrains the developing embryo and keeps it from growing. So you have to weaken the shell.

Scarification

Scarification is the general term for causing some physical change in the coating around a seed. The most basic method is filing or nicking it with a knife so that moisture can penetrate. Camelias are often treated to this beneficial abuse.

There are other forms of scarification that are helpful in penetrating the coating of the seed and, also, in giving it a leg up on absorbing moisture. The one that I prefer to knife-cutting seeds is dropping them in simmering water. That's *simmering*, not boiling, and indicates water temperatures of about 200°. As soon as you drop the seeds in the water, remove the pot from the heat and let them soak for twenty-four hours. The hot water breaks down the coating and the soaking starts the seed off right.

Even in cases where seeds don't need any form of scarification, they are often soaked overnight. This starts them on the road to germination quickly. However, if there is no hard shell that needs to be broken through, you don't have to use hot water. Just lukewarm tap water will do.

I should mention acid. Some nurseries use sulfuric acid to scarify seeds that have resistive coatings. They use sprays of the stuff and process huge numbers of seeds as they go. Don't even think about it. Forget it and if anyone suggests it think quietly to yourself, "This guy is nuts."

Berries

Berries are seeds with a layer of food stored around them that, ideally, decomposes into the soil around the seed and so is available upon germination. This food storage is call endosperm. Since you plan to feed your plants as soon as they need the food, you have no need for the endosperm. You'll have to remove it in order to germinate the seeds quickly. In such cases as Pyracantha or Holly, there's nothing very difficult about the process. Simply soak the seeds in water. After a while, the fleshy outer coating breaks down and floats to the surface. So too do any bad seeds. Brush the seeds periodically to remove the loosened berry material or rub them on a kitchen strainer. It takes only a day or so to remove all the pulp from the seeds.

Regardless of whether you use hot and cool water, it is a good idea to plant the seeds immediately after then have soaked. Seeds that get too wet or that are dried after they have begun to germinate will be damaged and die if not planted.

Planting

Except for the basics, planting seeds is a matter of tips, hints and suggestions that can be of help. But there's really very little to worry about. Seeds are designed to get along all by themselves under formidable circumstances. So long as you satisfy their simple needs, they germinate and grow. So, before getting into some of the more extreme forms of caution and assistance, here are the basics.

Soil

Seeds are usually rooted in the same kinds of mediums that are used for cuttings. They have the same requirements of air, moisture and, later, after leaves appear, nutrients. Seeds set very fragile roots just as cuttings do and so require the same constant moisture levels. Sand, vermiculite, perlite, sphagnum, peat moss and soil are all used as planting mediums. I use equal quantities by volume of sand, sphagnum and potting soil for the seeds I grow.

Perhaps the only special caution about mediums used in seed growth is that the seeds not be put in too acidic a soil unless they tend that way on their own. Rhododendron and Laurel like acidity. But most prefer neutral soils. If you are using peat moss, you should add a small quantity of powdered limestone to neutralize it and should look for the darkest-colored peat in the first place, as it is the most neutral.

Other than those few words of wisdom, you can follow the directions given under cuttings for soil.

Planting

Even if you are using very small containers for germinating seeds indoors, you should plant them in rows. This makes them easier to identify later on. You should use labels, even though you are sure you'll remember, because it's really hard to tell one cotyledon (seed leaf) from another. Planting in rows also makes the first transplanting easier. Some, like myself, with inherently sloppy minds and a distaste for regimentation, insist on scattering seeds. Scattering is wrong, wrong, wrong but I always do it this way.

Almost everybody has a different idea on how deep seeds should be planted. The key to the issue is a simple one, however, and is determined by the resources of the seed before it sets its first leaves. Until it does so, it has to exist on its stored foods. To make this as temporary a dependence as possible, you should plant seeds as shallowly as you dare, the only argument against simply pressing them into the soil being that they tend to dry out too quickly that way. I bury mine at a depth about twice their width. It seems to work.

Some years ago, when I was six, my father was planting something in the garden behind our house. Probably cucumbers. He was always planting cucumbers and radishes. Anyway, I was pestering around, dumping the wheelbarrow and stuff like that and he was giving me jobs to do, certainly in a well-considered effort to create the horticultural genius who is writing this thing. (Nice going, Dad). Where was I? Oh. Well, there he was with a package of what must have been cucumber seeds and there I was tipping over the wheelbarrow. So he gave me the package and asked me to arrange all the seeds right side up so that the roots wouldn't grow into the air and the leaves into the ground. I stared at those damn seeds looking for the feet for quite some time, quietly contemplating them. I gave up finally and asked, and he, with calm, paternal omniscience, explained to me that seeds have cats inside of them. And everybody knows that cats always fall on their feet. So, all you have to do is drop seeds onto the soil from a height of at least two inches and they automatically land right side up. I observed then and still observe that seeds and cats are governed by the inverse of the natural law that controls the falling of slices of bread with peanut butter on them. One always lands right side up, one right side down. Having carefully documented my source of information, I should now instruct you in the dropping of seeds: Hold them about two inches above the soil and let go. For the sceptics among you who don't think that there are cats in seeds, I can only retort that I have never grown a plant with its roots in the air. If it works, use it.

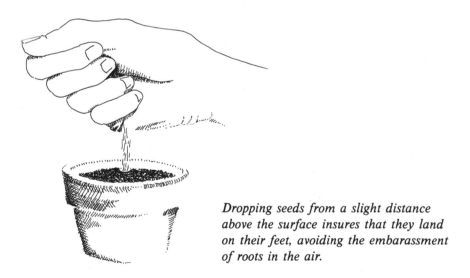

Dropping seeds from a slight distance above the surface insures that they land on their feet, avoiding the embarassment of roots in the air.

A Trick

After you have dropped your seeds and covered them, coat the surface of the medium with a thin layer of finely-ground sphagnum moss. I mince mine through a sieve. This stuff not only holds water but also retards the development of the fungi called damping off.

Another Trick

Before you plant your seeds, compact your soil fairly well and water it thoroughly. Do so, however, with ginger pats, not great, crunching pounds. As a rule, soil three inches deep should be pressed down about half an inch. Packing it any farther forces out the air pockets and greatly reduces the growth of your seedlings. Don't touch wet soil.

Watering thoroughly before the seeds are added allows you to get more water into the medium without the risk of washing the seeds around or uncovering them. If, after a week or two or three, the medium seems to be drying out, you can apply a fine mist of water to the top and add any more water by immersing the container from below.

Covering

After your seeds are planted, covered and watered, you should cover the container with a sheet of glass or plastic. This will hold water in for three weeks or so and you probably won't have to water again until leaves appear.

Hardening and Growth

The early stages of seedling growth are tenuous and sensitive. The new plants need ample supplies of water, should be given very diluted liquid fertilizers if they are growing in perlite or any other medium without soil, and must be given sunlight. This last is often delayed much too long. The only reason to keep seedlings out of the sun is to protect them from drying. If you cover the container with a plastic awning (not tightly, they need air as well), they can be grown in the sun. Much healthier seedlings will result.

Pricking Out

The first leaf or two that appears on the seedling is that earlier referred to as a cotyledon or seed leaf. These leaves are usually nondescript-looking things that don't resemble those of the mature plant. However, true leaves soon appear that look like the plant. When they do, you can, and probably should, transplant the seedlings. This first transplanting is called 'pricking out' and slows the growth of the plant temporarily. However, it also gives the roots room to develop and makes for a bushier plant because seedlings are allowed to spread rather than simply compete with each other.

In pricking out you have to be absurdly careful not to damage the new plant. Use a thin stick of some kind to unearth the roots and lift the plant by a leaf. (Grabbing it by the stem can crush the stem, killing the plant.) Replant immediately if not sooner. In resetting the seedlings, you can plant them deeper than they were growing in the seed bed so long as you don't bury any juncture of stems and leaves. Planting straight stems deeply causes them to produce roots and creates a dense, low plant. Burying the buds that exist at growing points near leaf and stem junctures may kill the plant.

The Second Transplanting

Should you have to retransplant the seedlings either outdoors or into pots, take a considerable amount of soil with the roots. Where the seed bed may have produced a few fine roots, requiring transplanting into soil with nutrients, the aftereffects of pricking out produces many more. Leave the soil around these.

Seed Containers

Seeds Indoors: Containers and Techniques

The requirements of seeds are very similar to those of cuttings.
They need just about the same kind of air, water, warmth and
mediums. But seeds are much smaller and produce initially smaller
plants. So a good number of them can be started in a very small
place and then pricked out as they begin to grow.

There are some classic lines that a writer on the subject of seed
germination is supposed to use at this point. For instance, the
mainstay of smalltime, amateur seed-growing is supposed to be the
Mason jar. I would venture to say that barely one in twenty of my
readers has a stock of Mason jars lying around. Putting things up for
the winter isn't as common as it used to be. So, I am not going to
suggest the use of Mason jars. Rather, I supply you with the
know-how to turn your basic peanut butter jar into a reasonable
facsimile. The other omnipresent container that writers claim to use
constantly (thereby proving their humility and readiness to use
what's at hand) is the coffee can. Everybody seems to think that
coffee cans are perfect for growing just about everything. Well, I'm
neither humble nor crazy about scrounging things. What I am is
poor. And when you're poor, you simulate humility almost by reflex.
So I tried coffee cans. They are too tall. There is no good reason for
putting so much medium under a seed. So, I use peanut butter jars
and small pieces of glass (explained below).

The Classic

When I intend to germinate only a few seeds, I use a small pot.
Nurseries use them in almost infinite quantity and infintesimal size. I
have six pretty small ones. I fill the pot with medium and press it
slightly. Generally, I then water it from below until it seems soaked.
Seeds are dropped on the top of the soil and covered either with

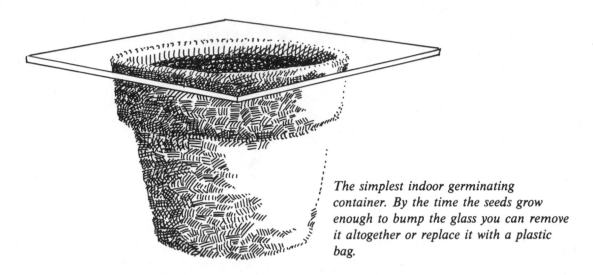

The simplest indoor germinating container. By the time the seeds grow enough to bump the glass you can remove it altogether or replace it with a plastic bag.

sand, vermiculite or a mixture of mediums including some soil. I mist this covering and sprinkle on a little sphagnum to keep the damping off to a minimum. Then I cover the whole works with a small piece of glass. The glass admits light and holds moisture very well. It's true that very little air is admitted and some people tell me that this slows the whole process. But, since my pots are chipped and gouged, there is ample air circulation. For those with new pots, try lifting the glass and saying hello once in a while. Usually the medium stays moist enough for germination to begin without further watering.

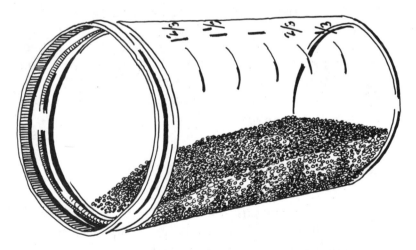

A peanut butter jar, even with its end open, makes a fine mini-hothouse for germinating seeds. Getting the seeds in and plants out is an interesting way to spend an afternoon.

And, some time before the seedlings bonk their heads on the glass, I remove it and either substitute a plastic tent or let the seedlings make it in the open air. Opening the container altogether makes careful scrutiny necessary, however, as drying out occurs faster. If I haven't stressed it enough up till now, I should say that drying out will, absolutely, kill very young seedlings. They have to be watched and kept moist.

The Sideways Greenhouse.

Another method of planting seeds is to put them in a glass jar lying on its side. This makes for some fussy work insofar as the scattering of seeds goes, but a knife or spoon does the trick. Punch several holes in the top of the jar and put the top on tightly. Here again, moisture stays in nicely until the plants are to be moved.

Pots You Can Plant

I've already mentioned, in the section on rooting containers, the use of pots that allow roots to grow through their sides. However, for trouble-free, easy-going seed germination, these pots can hardly be beat. Simply use them instead of a base of medium in flats and cold frames as discussed below.

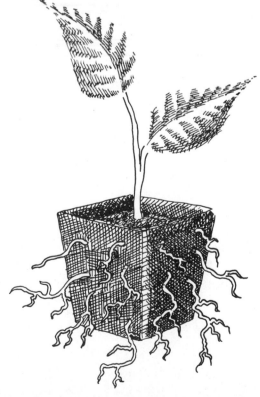

Flats

Flats is the name applied to a box small enough to be lifted when it is used in propagation. Here again you can refer to the section on rooting containers for more information. But there is a difference, at least a potential one, in the use of flats with seeds. Basically, seeds are shorter than cuttings. As a result, you don't have to build the tentlike structure over them that is required for cuttings.

Glass has always been a favorite covering for seeds planted in flats. Usually posts of some kind are propped in the corners of the flat and hold the glass a quarter-inch or so above the edge of the flat. This allows some air circulation. But you can use plastic sheeting just as well.

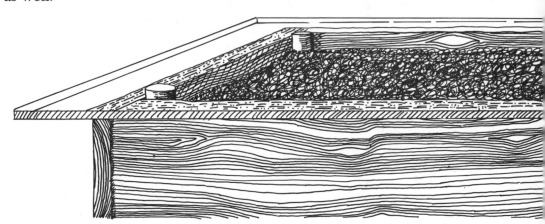

For some reason this drawing reminds me of Escher. I can't get my eyes to decide about which way the glass is. Anyway, it is supposed to be a flat with dowel posts in the corners. These posts hold the glass a quarter inch or so above the flat and allow some air circulation to the seeds.

General Notes.

Seed mediums are, as I mentioned before, about the same as those used for cuttings. However, most growers tend to apply a thicker mat of moss to the bottom of their flats when germinating seeds. They do this, perhaps, only because they don't have to insert a stem of any kind and don't have to worry about punching a hole in the moss to accept it. But it is also true that seeds generally lie very

118

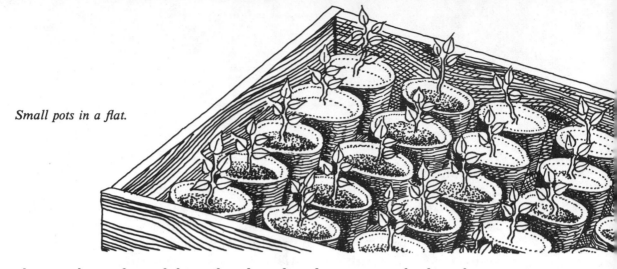

Small pots in a flat.

close to the surface of the soil and tend to dry more easily than the deeper-placed cuttings.

The other general point that I should make has to do with the use of cold frames and hotbeds with seed. What can I say? They work fine. I know that some people plant their seeds directly in soil placed in the frame, while others use flats or peat pots and put those in the frame. It doesn't seem to make much difference and you should make a distinction based only on convenience and the possibility that some seeds germinate much faster than others.

I am loathe to beat to death the variables of containers. So I'm going to stop here. I think that enough has been said about both the flexibility of containers and their general requirements to turn anyone with half a wit loose on the problem. So, rather than insult your intelligence, I suggest you look at the pictures and think hard. Good luck.

Seeds Outdoors

It's probably ironic, if looked at in the right way, that it has taken this much writing to get to the business of planting seeds in the ground. Seeds planted in the ground, after all, are Nature's major propagating method. But man has devised ways of playing around with this too, so I guess it's my responsibility to outline the techniques. But I do so with some trepidation. Throughout this book I've been talking about ways in which you can simulate and improve upon natural methods of reproducing plants. The techniques described here are adaptations of what may or may not happen in nature. The propagator and pirate simply select those circumstances that occur in nature and concentrate them on all his subjects. In this way, all the cuttings or seeds or layered parts have a good chance of making it. By means of plastic, glass, soil mixtures, temperature control, the proper choice of season and any number of other steps that can be taken, the plant-grower creates an environment that favors his plants. Nature might do this too. Or she might not.

119

I think that the instructions in this book offer a fairly broad spectrum of concern for your plants. I think that by now you should have a rather good idea of what they need to survive. But there is a threat that you will think that they need all of it, religiously applied, in order to make it. They don't. Should the temperature fail slightly or the moisture vary from the perfect, the chances are good that your plants will weather the trial. Very young seedlings may die. Or layerings may rot. Or some other catastrophe may occur. But the odds are with you. And this is especially true of seeds. They survive with grave stubbornness.

Consider, then, the following as an outline of suggestions. Aids to the natural. More or less preferred by the plants involved, not demanded by them. Remember too, that most of this book is like that.

Indoors/Outdoors

Cold frames and hotbeds have been mentioned several times in this book. I brought them up at the end of the preceding section on indoor seed growth because I'm not sure if frames should be considered an indoor or outdoor method. I'm mentioning them again here in order to hedge the issue.

However, there are a few more things I would like to say about them now. These techniques apply to the use of a frame in growing seeds or cuttings.

Some frames have wooden bottoms, a construction detail I've never understood since dirt is piled on top of the wood. But, regardless of that wooden bottom, several inches of porous soil are added and compacted rather firmly. This is not the soil that holds the cuttings or seeds. It is simply a large, substantial reservoir of moisture and a drainage convenience. This soil mixture is then watered very thoroughly, to the verge of wetness, that is, supermoist.

Most growers then put peat pots or flats on top of the soil and it is in these that the seeds do their actual growing. I strongly suggest this technique. You can grow directly in the frame if you wish, but that makes applying the seeds more difficult, makes organizing them a chore and makes pricking out harder. Some seeds come up much faster than others and it's a good idea to be able simply to lift a small flat out of the frame and work on it without disturbing anything else that goes on in there.

With this system, note that there are actually two bodies of soil: the one at the bottom of the frame and one in the flats or peat pots. The base soil helps keep the atmosphere moist inside the frame. So, when watering, be sure to keep both damp. They are both important.

One of the major advantages of growing seeds in frames outdoors is that the process of hardening off can be approached gradually and in one place. 'Hardening off' is the expression used to describe the maturing of the seedling. As the seedling begins to photosynthesize and produce leaves characteristic of its variety, you should begin to allow more and more air circulation around the plant. This not only aids photosynthesis but also lowers the temperature inside the frame, getting the plant ready for the real world. Frames with hinged window sashes are usually propped up progressively higher. At the same time, shading is reduced.

Outdoors/Outdoors

Sowing seeds outdoors is as much gardening as it is propagation. But there are a few basic requirements that can be handled within the scope of this book and so I'll pass them along in terse fashion. If you would like to know more about any of the many issues that are left up in the air, try reading a more general text on gardening.

Germinating seeds in the ground requires the sort of soil that the mature plant will need. This, in its most advanced forms, can become a meticulous mania requiring endless soil adjustments. The opposite approach is merely to scratch the soil and plant. Ever-adhering to the golden mean of moderation, I take a course somewhere in the middle, neither fussing overmuch with the dirt nor ignoring the seed's requirements. My approach may seem a matter of some overkill to many people, but the fact of the matter is that I enjoy the job, so the relative value of the work that goes into it is meaningless. I get what I really want by doing it all in the first place, not so much by the success of the plants. Though that's nice too.

The soil itself is probably the single most important thing in outdoor gardening. Improving what you've got isn't hard, as you can till it slightly and let it go at that. But, if you plan to use the same plot for any period of time, you might try going all the way. There are any number of fine books specifically for perrenials, vegetables, herbs, shrubs, trees, bulbs, etc., that offer all kinds of soil advice. And there are some fine books available on organic gardening that either help or interest you. Here, however, are some basic techniques that can help you regardless of the plants involved.

Double Digging

In spite of the fact that double digging is just what it sounds like, it needs some explanation anyway. You dig into your garden about eight to ten inches and pile that soil to one side. Then you dig another eight to ten inches and pile that soil to the other side. Then you take the first pile and throw it into the hole. Then you throw the second pile in. While you're at it, you can remove large rocks, add compost and correct the pH balance of the soil as well. Double digging is a lot of work. But it greatly improves the bed and serves as an ideal framework for the rest of the procedures suggested here.

Compost and Drainage

As I mentioned before, lots of good things have been suggested in print about the improvement of soil. Any natural or organic gardening book describes for you the ins and outs of composting. However, I would like to say that compost piles are fun. You can play the witch and brew to your heart's content with coffee grounds, egg shells and salad remains. You can also become highly mechanized, (buy a shredder from Sears), very chemical (buy compost accelerating additives from nurseries) and amaze your friends by forcing them to put their hands on the compost pile in order to feel for themselves the heat therein generated. But what you mostly get is decomposed stuff for soil improvement.

The other material often added to soil is sand. You follow the same considerations as go into the preparation of potting and rooting mixtures and try to supply the soil with drainage. Clean construction sand that is free of salt does the trick and greatly improves even the most claylike soil.

pH and Fertilizer

This last step may take some practice because you can't always make ample corrections at the time of double digging. But it doesn't matter, since you can apply lime or sulfur later and water it in. The pH of a substance is a measurement of its alkalinity or acidity. Plants prefer different balances between sweet and acid soil and you should consult your trusty encyclopedia on this. But, generally, pH is measured on a scale from 0 to 14, with 7 (usually expressed as 7.0 in order to impress those impressed by accuracy) representing a neutral balance. Perhaps the most important thing to remember about these pH numerical measurements is that they are not linear. 6.0 is a slightly acid rating. 8.0 is a slightly alkaline one. But 5.0 is ten times more acid than 6.0 and 4.0 is 100 times more acid. This can be very important if you send soil samples to your state's agricultural department or take it to a local nursery for testing. This geometric progression makes correction a trial and error process that you have to learn to live with.

To lower the pH of your soil, you add sulfur. This makes it more acid. Generally, in a plot containing 50 square feet, you should start with between 1/4 and 1/2 pound of sulfur. If the correction isn't sufficient, add a little more. To raise the pH (make it more alkaline), add powdered limestone. More lime is needed per square foot for correction than sulfur, about one pound for every 10 to 20 square feet.

I'm also going to offer a short paragraph on fertilizer. But only as an introduction. First, don't apply strong fertilizers to seeds or young seedlings. Second, fertilize minimally if you have composted your soil. Finally, buy fertilizers with rather well-balanced numerical ratings. Those that are very heavy in any one element can be 'hot' and overfeed your plants to death. The numbers I'm talking about here are marked on the bag in which the fertilizer comes, such as 5–10–5. The first numeral represents the amount of nitrogen, the second, phosphate and the last, potash. These are basic requirements of any plant and are balanced in any mixture, depending upon the soil to which it is applied. Ask at your local nursery about your soil, if you want, and try sending some to the agricultural department of your state's largest university. They can suggest proper correction.

Planting

After you have corrected the soil to your heart's content, rake it lightly. The idea here isn't to powder the soil because that greatly limits the amount of air in it. Rather, raking should leave lumps, noticeable amounts of organic matter and remove stones.

Next, dig or hoe one or two-inch deep trenchlets for your seeds. (Check the seed packages for depth instructions.) There is one important note here that I should make. Plant in straight rows. This makes weeding easier, makes identifying what you've grown much more simple and makes your garden look like one of those aerial photos of the Midwest. I've a good friend who recently planted his first garden. As he is a very good friend and fine person, I will call him Bobby. Anyway, Bobby is from Jersey City and had never considered planting a vegetable garden before. When he did so, he followed his nose, planting this way and that and ending with a set of patches that couldn't be identified easily. In the first thinning out he eliminated the carrots altogether, I think, and as he went along, he slowly butchered most of what he was trying to grow in favor of some lovely and vigorous weeds. So it goes. I remember, after it was too late to do anything about it, watching him trample the radishes as he tried to get to the cucumbers. I also remember the stakes he set up for the beans only to find that the pumpkins were growing on them.

Cover seeds firmly but not tightly. Mist them with a fine spray and wait. Water them regularly until they have germinated and begun to harden and then water them some more as you see fit.

After the seeds have germinated, you'll probably have to thin them out. Ruthlessly select the largest and most healthy of the seedlings and either discard or transplant the rejects.

Auxiliary Techniques

There are, of course, threats to your seedlings that will prevail over the methods described above. Rabbits, deer, insects and too much sun or not enough moisture will seriously damage seedlings. But, as I mentioned before, I don't want to oversell the care and feeding of seeds. Rather, I offer a few directions in which you can head.

Tents

Most mail-order nurseries sell small plastic tents that can be erected over seeds in order to keep the atmosphere around them both moist and insect free.

Fences and mothballs

Both discourage animals.

Division

Division, as I'm using it here at least, is a kind of catchall word that describes all sorts of asexual propagation. It differs from the others discussed in this book by being a mixture of them. That is, the grab bag of division techniques involves the skills and techniques found in most other kinds of propagation. But division is almost never as extreme a form. You don't divide something unless the part that you end up with has some amount of root and above-ground growth. But the techniques involved in root cuttings or stem cuttings are essential to division. So too is an appreciation of the trauma of being torn apart. So just about every sympathy that you develop in other methods is part of your job in division. But not to such a thorough degree. And, in a way, that brings us back to transplanting. In division you transplant parts of plants, each having at least some roots and, if not actually foliage, at least the buds to produce them.

Having all the elements of a real plant, a divided piece is in a much better position than a single part that is asked to differentiate beyond itself. All the makings of a plant are there, all you need do is protect and encourage it. And this is probably the only hard and fast distinction between division and everything else: that you have to be careful to include both roots and buds in the part you intend to grow. The skill involved in doing so is a matter of recognizing divisible units within a plant. There are those plants that quite naturally 'divide' in the sense of producing clusters of themselves that can be easily broken apart. And it is these that usually are treated to this technique. Their growth suggests division, and, since it's easier, you usually prefer it to cuttings, layering or whatever.

In dividing anything, you have to remember that the plant depends on the good condition of its roots to survive. Separating roots that are tangled and grown together should be done gently. Breaking a few doesn't kill most plants, but it slows them. Similarly, if the top growth of the plant is tangled and difficult to separate, remember to try and leave each of the divided root structures with a small but complete set of foliage parts. If you keep that in mind and go slowly, you'll be able to find what's needed for the generation of a plant and separate it from the whole.

To forewarn you, there are situations coming up shortly where it will seem that a full deck of cards hasn't really been left to the divided part. Well, yes and no. Bear with me for simplicity's sake and I'll try to explain my reasoning as we go along.

Generally, plants are divided when dormant. That makes sense in light of the appreciable shock that chopping up involves. Dormant division in the fall or very early spring allows the plant to set roots and establish top growth in accordance with its root supply. As in transplanting, this period of dormancy provides a lull in the demands the plant is making on itself and so allows it to concentrate its first energies on growing those parts it needs to survive.

Dividing isn't as easy as these pictures might make you think. Gently separating the roots is easy enough, but there's a lot of dirt that crumbles and falls all over the place. Which leads me to the conclusion that cleaning up is harder than dividing.

Suckers

A sucker is a shoot that grows out of the root system of a plant from below ground. It is actually just another stem or branch of the plant but is attached directly to its root system. This attachment allows you to separate the sucker from the plant and leave some of the roots attached to it.

A sucker is removed by digging around it, finding a logical division point between the main root system and that which is producing the sucker and then cutting the two apart. Sometimes the roots left on the sucker are substantial, sometimes not. Depending on this very point, you should treat the new plant with the kind of pampering you would show a newly-rooted cutting. Supply it with water, some light, shelter and food. Before long it will develop the roots necessary to live well on its own.

Suckers appear on all sorts of trees and shrubs. They are usually the result of vitality and are almost always fast-growing parts of the plant. You don't have to fret over them as you might over a stem cutting but recognize that they may be suffering from a diminished supply from their roots.

Crowns

A crown is another kind of unit within a single plant that invites division. Plants like African Violet and many ferns grow stems from central, ground-level cores. The place where the stems converge is called a crown. And most of these plants mature by growing additional crowns, sometimes several on a single potted plant.

These crowns are a viable unit within the plant. It was noted earlier in the book that African Violet crowns can be cut off at

Divide Sansevieria when it seems to be exploding from the pot. Cut large hunks of root with a sharp knife.

ground level and rooted in water. They can also be divided by using a razor to separate the crowns and then using your fingers to divide the roots. You end up with a bunch of small African Violets that have root systems attached. This makes them easy to plant and much more difficult to kill.

Simple Division

Every other form of simple division involves plants that have less neatly-defined units within themselves. Crowns and suckers are special cases that dictate the form of the division. Other plants grow many shoots which are independent at ground level. That is, they come out of the ground one at a time or in small bunches. All these shoots come from a single root structure but each stem is more closely associated with some roots than with others. Sansevieria is probably the most often divided plant. The many vertical leaves of it make for straightforward division. You simply take a bunch of leaves and pull them from the rest. Be careful, though, with any division of this kind. In Sansevieria and Aspidistra both, the roots wrap around each other and can be damaged in the separating. Whenever possible, use your fingers, not a pitchfork, to divide the tangled roots of plants. You're less likely to be cruel to them this way.

Plants like Day Lilies can be divided the same way indoor plants are. Simply split them at the roots. But more substantial roots, such as those on Peonies, have to be divided with a knife or cutter. Again, in making the division, try to find logical units to the root structure, places where it can be divided most simply. Also, take care to preserve as many of the smallest root hairs as possible. It's these that do the bulk of the drinking.

Bulbs, Corms, Tubers and Rhizomes

In most texts, this kind of division is put in a chapter all by itself, quite separated from talk of Peonies and African Violets. But, to my mind, the means of propagating them are very similar. In fact, they only differ by degree. In the division techniques described above, a fairly substantial amount of above-ground growth goes along with the process. Even in the case of Peonies, the stems are there even if the flowers and foliage have gone by. But the division of bulbs is different, in an odd way, and corms, tubers and rhizomes are very different. I'll explain.

Bulbs

A bulb appears to be a root for no other reason than it lives below ground. But it's not. A bulb is a tight bunch of scales, like leaves, that grow on a base plate (called a basil plate) and from which roots grow. A bulb, then, is the central part of the plant, used to store energy and produce above-ground growth and roots.

Many bulbs divide themselves naturally by simply producing small bulblike offshoots called, aptly, bulblets. Tulips do this very readily. In the case of bulbs that propagate themselves, all you have to do is separate the distinct bulb units. Plant them and they'll grow.

Others don't produce these bulblets so readily. But you can force them. There are two techniques, both pretty much the same, that involve the scarring or removal of the basil plate from the bulb. Turn it upside down and either scoop out all of the basil plate (thereby removing any roots as well) or take a knife to the plate, carving an asterisk in it. I prefer the scooping method because it

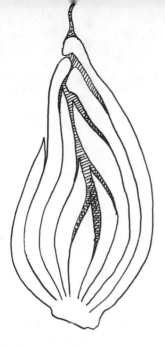

A cutaway view of a tulip bulb.

produces more bulblets. I use a spoon that I've sharpened with a file but lots of propagators use melon-ballers and some simply dig away with a knife.

Regardless of technique, you leave the bulb upside down and store it in a warm place for a few months (over the winter). Come spring, you plant the bulb, with the developing bulblets still attached, and let it grow a season. When fall rolls around again you'll find that the bulblets have grown considerably and can be broken off from the main and planted on their own. They are small, however, and will probably take two or three years at least to produce flowers.

After you've stimulated bulbs or simply found bulbs that have propagated on their own, keep in mind that dividing them is a form of division. In cutting them from the main, you should try to take the central core of the bulb scales, the basil plate associated with it and any buds and roots that are attached. This unit constitutes a complete plant in dormant form. See, I told you it was division.

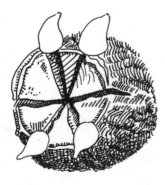

The basil plate of this bulb has been both removed and cut with a knife. The bulblets appear after a winter's storage in a warm place and will grow larger when planted (the bulb still upside down) for the summer.

131

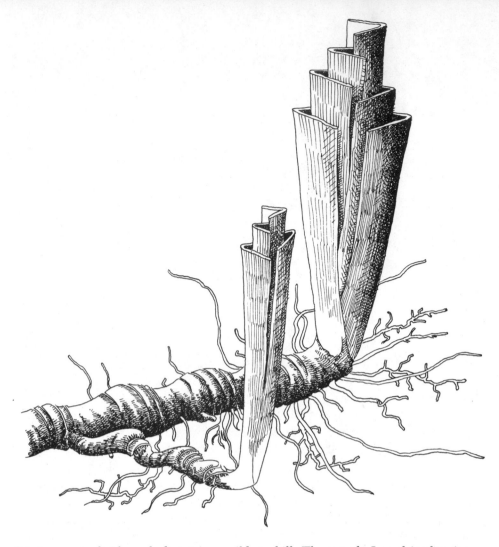

Iris is easy to divide and almost impossible to kill. The sample I used in drawing this picture grew in the woods behind my parents' home where my mother threw a pile of garden garbage. Note that the leaves are cut back when dividing and transplanting.

Corms, Tubers and Rhizomes

This trio differs from bulbs in not being composed of scales. They are roots. All three are food-storage facilities and tend to propagate themselves.

I consider the separating of these root systems to be division because they contain buds. In fact, each must contain a bud when separated from the main plant. This isn't very hard and you'll find that in the likes of Gladiolus or Begonia, the buds are easy to find at the upper end of the root.

Dividing these energy-rich roots is relatively easy. They contain incredible amounts of reserve foodstuffs for the subsistence of the plant until it is established. But, as in any kind of division, you should

132

try to retain any small root hairs that you can. If you break them off, they'll only have to be regrown.

The only point here is to be very careful in cutting the discrete portions of the roots apart so that each ends up with a bud or 'eye.' In the case of such radical surgery as that perpetrated on the likes of Begonias, this can be tricky and you should be careful. And, when the cuts made in dividing them are at all large, you should treat the exposed cut with a fungicide of some kind so that it heals well.

That's about all there is to it. Plant bulbs, corms, tubers and rhizomes just as you would the mature plant. Treat them to a little care and watering at first, but not too much, and they will thrive and grow very quickly.

Lights & Mist

This chapter deals with two of the more peripheral areas of advanced propagation insanity. Not insane because they are outrageously expensive or time-consuming, nor because they require a supreme dedication to the pastime, but because they are rare and somewhat specialized, require a consistent level of commitment and tend to elicit weird looks and odd conversation from neighbors and friends behind the backs of their owners and users. Mist especially, but, to some extent, lights too, when used in propagation.

Imagine, if you will, the apparently justified bewilderment of a neighbor who, for one reason or another, has stumbled into your basement. There, in the corner, is a large box on legs or a series of trays and in these trays is dirt. Above the dirt hang two bulbs burning away. "Reading lights for bookworms?" "Are you warming the dirt or trying to give it a tan?" There are other possible quips, none up to Johnny Carson quality, and none that make me laugh anymore. I'm tired of being persecuted for my foibles. I'm tired of being made fun of and whispered about because I shine light on dirt. I confess that, in part, this book is a defense against such slurs.

So, to silence my gossipy neighbors and calm my wife, I've decided to write a little about lights and mist even though most of you may not be interested much.

Lights

The sun is the best of all possible sources of light for germinating and growing plants. If you have the space and the inclination, build a cold frame outside and do your propagating there. If, however, you want to work inside, you'll have to supply your plants with artificial sources.

Artificial light is most useful in starting seeds and for rooting or growing young plants. It gives you a head start on summer. It's also not a very expensive addition to your gardening equipment. About $50 can set you up with the lights and timer that you need.

Plants vary in respect to the amount and kinds of light they need. Most operate naturally on a photo-period of between 12 and 15 hours. That is how long they must be exposed to the source for healthy growth. Some require more, some less. Seeds generally appreciate more, up to 18 hours, and some light-sensitive seeds absolutely require light to germinate.

There are many kinds of bulbs sold as lighting for plants. However, the best are florescent and incandescent, which can be used alone or, for best results, in conjunction with one another. Florescent lights tend to affect a plant's photosynthetic process, its ability to take in and manufacture products. Incandescent bulbs have a greater influence on the growth rates of plants such as the length and curves of stems. These two functions clearly do not exist independently. Nor does one sort of light ignore the other need. But this more or less represents the balance of each source's influence.

Lights for Seeds

Extensive reading in the use of artificial lighting can get you involved in a complex array of foot-candle equations for a multitude of different purposes. But, without a light meter and a good deal of knowledge about the needs of different plants, such measurements are of little or no use. Not being particularly interested in numbers, I try to keep those with which I deal to a minimum. So I've devised two simple rules for germinating seeds under lights that work almost all the time.

First, it seems only logical to me that there is little or no sense in shining lights on covered seeds. On the other hand, some seeds won't germinate unless almost entirely covered. So, I spread the seeds and cover them loosely with soil. Then I water them with a very fine spray until the seeds just begin to show through the dirt. Then I turn on the lights and wait.

I use the common formula for indoor lights and seeds: about 10 watts per square foot of medium about 10 inches from the soil. (Note the clever duplication of the number ten in order to aid a shaky memory). I also use both incandescent and florescent lights on seeds. Many propagators tell me that the incandescent bulb isn't really necessary but I feel that its warmth helps in my cold cellar.

Lights for Seedlings, Plants and Cuttings

Generally, double the wattage for plants, etc. This isn't a hard and fast rule, however. Some seedlings need to be nursed along for a while as they make the transition from their earlier reduced lighting. And some cuttings may wilt if too much light is applied too fast. Of course, you can adjust light very precisely if you have mounted them on pulleys. Simply raise the bulbs to reduce the light. Don't adjust the quantity of light by adjusting the number of hours that plants are exposed. This kind of confusion can damage plants.

Working with artificial light isn't nearly as difficult as it might seem. But you can't expect this sort of introduction to tell you what you need to know. Here I bow to superior authorities and suggest you pick up a book on the subject, if you are interested. Carry with you a proper disdain for what seems to be nit-picking and an open mind about proper advice. Most of all, pay attention to your plants, and they will make every effort to tell you when you are doing something wrong.

Mist

The idea behind the use of mist in the propagation of cuttings is perfect. And the results are almost as good. But the equipment required is a little frightening, and not cheap either. However, some improvements have been made in this area and I think that I may try it soon. So far I've only watched the operation of a nursery set-up with longing and admiration for the ease of rooting that results from using mist in rooting difficult cuttings.

In order to try mist, you need either a greenhouse or some sort of semi-enclosed space outdoors. It's just too wet for the cellar. It's this space requirement that has held me back so far, but as the equipment being produced becomes more and more adjustable, I think that I may soon be able to operate a 'fog box' on a small scale. But this probably isn't the place to be talking myself into anything, so, on to the theory.

Traditionally, cuttings have been rooted in greenhouses or cold frames with some sort of lathing or cheesecloth to limit the amount of light they receive. Even with the use of polyethylene, you still have to watch carefully and control the light that falls on the cuttings. Too much sun simply wilts and then kills them. The unfortunate part of this limitation is that the more sun and air that can be allowed to reach the cuttings, the more active they will be and so the faster they will root.

The solution to this problem has been a matter of trading off light and moisture. Even with the highly-moist enclosures of poly tents and cold frames, there has been a limitation in the levels of moisture that could be maintained. And, the more thorough the moisture seal, the less air could circulate. Certainly the resulting environment for the cuttings was and is very acceptable, but not the best. And I think I should say that the best may not make any sense. Amateurs like us, with carefully bridled hopes and no need for quantity production on a fast schedule, probably need have nothing to do with mist. Its major benefit is saving time, with the related ability to root greater proportions of attempted cuttings before they die. I've already ranted about how little I think either you or I should be concerned with the percentage of successes we experience. And by now you should know me well enough to guess what I think of the importance of saving a week or two. But I'm fascinated by the surreal approach of misting and the remarkable results it achieves with some very difficult rootings. So, here's how it works.

There are two types of mist, one that operates constantly and one that is used indoors. Constant mist is an outdoor operation. An enclosure is set up, usually with four-foot-high walls of canvas and cuttings are put in it in flats. Then a high-pressure nozzle is directed into this enclosure and constantly bathes the foliage of the cuttings with a very fine mist of water. Full sunlight is allowed and air circulation, if not wind, is okay. The mist in the 'fog box' prevents wilting.

A problem lies in the extraordinary drainage requirements of the medium. Since water is constantly being poured on it, there is a problem with air getting to the roots. The ingenious solution to the problem was to turn the mist off once in a while. This technique is called intermittent mist and involves a three second spray every minute or so.

Both systems require timers because no mist is applied at night even in the constant mist method. But the additional timing of the intermittent mist allows the soil to stay a little drier and a little warmer too. Both aid in rooting. Intermittent misting is also versatile. As the cuttings begin to root and need to be gradually hardened for transplanting, the periods between mistings or the duration of them can be changed to reduce the amount of water.

The newest of the many forms of mist control is really clever and I can't resist telling you about it. This set-up is for sale through several mail-order houses and costs from $100 to $150.00, depending on the optional stuff you get. The machine works on the theory that the amount of time between mistings isn't actually important to the cuttings. In fact, what matters is that they stay moist. So this mister has a little screen that catches mist just like the leaves do. When the screen gets wet, it gets heavy and drops, throwing a switch that turns off the mist. As the leaves begin to dry, so does the screen, which, in turn, lifts, turning the water back on. Nifty.

Well, that's all I know about mist and artificial light. So, that's all there is to this chapter.

Conclusion

That's just about all there is to this book. There remains an index of plants and propagation methods, but that's it. Not much in the way of prose and so little chance to try again to give you the feel of making plants grow from the parts of plants. I guess I've done about all that I can do.

So, I'm finished. I know that I am supposed to be slightly elated at this point, that I am supposed to sit back and fold my arms and smile the smile of the satisfied. Or I'm supposed to say 'Whoopee' as though school were out. But that's not at all the way I feel. Funny, isn't it? But I really liked writing this, so much so that if anybody buys this book, I'm going to do it again. It was definitely fun. In fact, if you enjoyed reading it half as much as I did writing it, then I'm sure you loved every word.

Well, the only thing I have to say now is something that I can't remember ever seeing in a book. And I don't know why. Maybe because most people don't think of books in the conversational way I think of them. Or maybe it's taken for granted. Or maybe people think of books all wrong. Take this one for instance. It cost $3.95 ($6.95 in the super duper hardbound edition). Not so much, really. So little, in fact, it clearly has nothing to do with what went into it. I wouldn't draw the pictures or write the words for that. And you wouldn't spend the time you've spent reading it if you didn't get something worth more than four bucks. So there's an odd, uneconomical relationship here that I've been thinking about. And my part of it boils down to thanking you for being patient and not interrupting me as I went along. I appreciate it beyond the portion of your $3.95 that will eventually find its way to me. So, here, for the first time anywhere in a book of any kind whatsoever is a thank you.

The Index

This part of the book is probably a little confusing to those of you who have read everything up to this point. You may remember that I said a couple of times that there would be no grand index of plants and propagation methods. And now you get to the end and find there is a grand (at least big) index of plants and propagation methods. Well, one of the privileges of being a self-published author is that you can change your mind. So, in spite of all the sensible and still good reasons for not including an index like the one that follows, I'm going to do it anyway.

But I would like to explain why. You see, after the first printing of this book a couple of friends and a younger sister had the nerve to tell me that I was wrong about indices. They argued that to omit one was to leave out the reinforcing assurance most people need before they start hacking away at their plants. And, it was explained to me, everybody wasn't nutty enough to shell out $15 or $20 for an encyclopedia of plants. It would be nice, they said, if I gave people a little help.

So that's what I've done.

But this index of plants isn't much like those you're likely to find in other books. First of all, it was a pain to put together. I made a list of the plants I am familiar with and then added a few that I knew others grow. I then asked a bunch of friends what they thought and I consulted several nursery people. One person told me to include Frangipani for the sake of the name. And another suggested Elm because the Elms are all dying and if enough people propagate them maybe one will show up that is resistant to the disease. Everybody had a weird reason for something or other. So, generally speaking, I included everything that I could find out.

Another oddity of the following index is its listings. I can never remember the generic names of plants. *Aspidistra* is always Abigail to me and *Sansevieria* is always Snake Plant. So I've listed everything twice, once by its common name and once by its official, unpronounceable, italicized name. Look things up either way.

And there is one more thing. I have listed every method of pirating that has been reported to me from some reasonably reliable source. Obviously, some methods listed for a plant will work better than others. So, I would suggest you start with cuttings if in doubt. If that doesn't work, try another method.

House Plants

The Plants	Softwood cuttings	Hardwood cuttings	Root cuttings	Division	Layering	Grafting	Budding	Offsets	Seed	Stratification	Comments
Abutilon (Flowering Maple)	•								•		
Acacia (Mimosa)	•	•							•		Soak seeds overnight.
Acalypha hispida (Chenille Copperleaf)	•										
Achimenes (Achimenes)	•			•							
Acorus (Japanese Sweet Flag)				•							
Adiantum (Maidenhair Fern)				•				•			Spores.
Aechmea (Bromeliad)		•									Cuttings of suckers.
Aeonium (Succulents)		•						•			
African Hemp (Sparrmania)											
African Violet (Saintpaula)	•			•							Divide multi-crowned plants.
African Lily (Agapanthus)				•							
Agapanthus (African Lily)				•							
Agave americana (Century Plant)	•										Cuttings of suckers.
Aglaonema modestum (Chinese Evergreen)	•			•							

Plant		Cuttings of suckers.
Air Plant (*Kalanchoe pinnata*)		
Aloe (Aloe)		
Alternanthera (Alternanthera)		
Aluminum Plant (*Pilea cadierei*)		
Amaryllis (*Hippeastrum*)		
Anthurium (Anthurium)		
Aphelandra (Aphelandra)		
Aporocactus (Rat Tail Cactus)		
Aralia, False (*Dizygotheca elegantissima*)		
Arrowhead Plant (*Sagittaria*)		
Arrowroot (*Maranta*)		
Artillery Plant (*Pilea microphylla*)		
Araucaria excelsa (Norfolk Island Pine)		
Asparagus Fern (*Asparagus*)		
Aspidistra (Cast Iron Plant)		
Asplenium (Spleenwort)		
Asplenium nidus (Bird's Nest Fern)		
Astrophytum (Star Cactus)		
Avocado (*Persea americana*)		

The Plants	Softwood cuttings	Hardwood cuttings	Root cuttings	Division	Layering	Grafting	Budding	Offsets	Seed	Stratification	Comments
Bamboo (*Arundinaria,*	•	•									
Bambusa,	•	•	•	•							
Phyllostachys)			•								
Begonia (*Begonia*)	•										
Begonia, Tuberous (*Begonia*)	•		•								
Bellflower (*Campanula*)				•				•			
Beloperone (Shrimp Plant)	•		•								
Billbergia (Bromeliad)	•		•					•			
Bird's Nest Fern (*Asplenium nidus*)			•								
Bird of Paradise (*Strelitzia reginae*)			•					•			
Bloodleaf (*Iresine*)	•										
Boston Fern (*Nephrolepis exaltata*)			•								
Bougainvillea (*Bougainvillea*)	•										
Brake Fern (*Pteris*)			•					•			
Bromeliad (*Aechmea*)	•										
Bromeliad (*Billbergia*)	•							•			
Bryophyllum (Chandelier Plant)	•										Bulbils at leaves.
Burro Tail (*Sedum morganianum*)	•		•					•			

Caladium (Caladium)	•	•		
Calathea (Calathea)		•	•	
Calceolaria (Calceolaria)	•			
Calla (Zantedeschia)	•			
Campanula (Bellflower)	•	•		
Cape Primrose (Streptocarpus)	•	•	•	
Capsicum (Christmas Pepper)	•			
Carex (Sedge)		•		
Carissa (Natal Plum)	•		•	
Cast Iron Plant (Aspidistra)		•		
Century Plant (Agave americana)			•	
Cephalocereus (The Old Man Cactus)			•	
Ceropegia (Rosary Plant)		•		
Chandelier Plant (Bryophyllum)			•	Bulbils at leaves.
Chenille Plant (Acalypha hispada)			•	
Chinese Evergreen (Aglaonema modestum)		•	•	
Chlorophytum elatum (Spider Plant)		•	•	Cuttings of plantlets.
Christmas Pepper (Capsicum)	•		•	
Chrysanthemum (Chrysanthemum)	•	•	•	
Cineraria (Senecio cruentus)	•	• •	•	

The Plants	Softwood cuttings	Hardwood cuttings	Root cuttings	Division	Layering	Grafting	Budding	Offsets	Seed	Stratification	Comments
Cissus (Treebine & Grape Ivy)	●										
Citrus (Dwarf Lemon & Orange)					●	●					
Cliff Brake (Pellaea)			●					●			
Clivia (Kafir Lily)			●								
Clock Vine (Thunbergia)	●										
Coccoloba (Sea Grape)	●			●				●			
Codiaeum (Croton)	●										
Coleus (Coleus)	●										
Columnea (Columnea)	●										
Cordyline (Dracena)	●			●				●			
Croton (Codiaeum)	●										
Cryptanthus (Earth Stars)	●										
Cyclamen (Cyclamen)								●			
Cyperus alternifolius (Umbrella Plant)	●										
Davallia (Hare's Foot Fern)			●								
Dieffenbachia (Dumb Cane, Tuftfoot)	●										
Dizygotheca (Threadleaf, False Aralia)	●										

Dracaena (Dracena)	●	●	●			
Dracena (Cordyline)						
Dragon Tree (Dracaena draco)						
Duchesnea indica (Mock Strawberry)						
Dumb Cane (Dieffenbachia)						
Earth Stars (Cryptanthus)						
Echeveria (Echeveria)	●					
Echinocactus (Gold Ball Cactus)						
Episcia (Peacock)						
Euphorbia pulcherrima (Poinsettia)						
Fatshedera (Fatshedera)						
Fatsia (Fatsia)						
Ferns (Pteris,	Spores.					
Polypodium,	Spores.					
Nephrolepis,	Spores.					
Adiantum,	Spores.					
Humata)	Spores.					
Ficus (Fig, Rubber Plant)						

The Plants	Softwood cuttings	Hardwood cuttings	Root cuttings	Division	Layering	Grafting	Budding	Offsets	Seed	Stratification	Comments
Fiddle Leaf Fig (*Ficus lyrata*)	●			●							
Fig (*Ficus*)	●	●		●							
Flowering Maple (*Abutilon*)	●								●		
Fortunella (*Kumquat*)					●	●			●		
Foxtail (*Setaria*)			●						●		
Fuchsia (*Fuchsia*)	●								●		Dry seeds over the winter.
Gelsemium sempervivens (Jessamine)	●								●		
Geranium (*Pelargonium*)	●										
Gloxinia (*Sinningia*)	●								●		
Gold Ball Cactus (*Echinocactus*)	●										
Grape Ivy (*Cissus*)	●										
Gynura (Velvet Plant)	●								●		
Hare's Foot Fern (*Davallia*)				●							
Hedera (Ivy)	●				●	●			●		
Heliotrope (*Heliotropium*)	●			●					●		
Hibiscus (Hibiscus)	●	●		●	●				●		

Hippeastrum (Amaryllis)	●●	
Houseleek (*Sempervivum*)	●	
Hoya (Wax Plant)		Propagate by scoring bulbs.
Hyacinthus (Hyacinth)	●	
Hydrangea (Hydrangea)	●	
Impatiens (Patience Plant, Snapweed)	●	
Iresine (Bloodleaf)		
Iron Plant (*Aspidistra*)		
Ivy (*Hedera*)	●	
Ivy-arum (*Scindapsus*)		
Jade Plant (*Crassula*)		
Japanese Maple (*Acer palmatum*)	●●	Stratify seeds for 4 months at about 40°.
Jasminum (Jasmine)	●	
Java Fig (*Ficus bejamina*)		
Jerusalem Cherry (*Solanum pseudocapsicum*)	●	
Jessamine (*Gelsemium sempervivens*)	●	
Kafir Lily (*Clivia*)		

The Plants	Softwood cuttings	Hardwood cuttings	Root cuttings	Division	Layering	Grafting	Budding	Offsets	Seed	Stratification	Comments
Kalanchoe (Kalanchoe,	●										Propagate through bulbils on leaves.
Airplant,	●										Propagate through bulbils on leaves.
Pandaplant	●										Propagate through bulbils on leaves.
Kangaroo Treebine (*Cissus antarctica*)	●										
Lantana (Lantana)	●							●			
Laurel, Sweet Bay (*Laurus nobilis*)		●						●			
Lemon Tree, Dwarf (*Citrus*)						●					
Lilium (Lily)				●			●	●			Bulbils form on stem and leaves, or divide offshoots or bulb scales.
Maidenhair Fern (*Adiantum*)				●				●			Spores.
Maranta (Arrowroot, Prayer Plant)				●				●			
Medinilla (Medinilla)	●										
Mimosa (*Acacia*)	●		●					●			
Mock Strawberry (*Duchesnea indica*)				●							
Monstera deliciosa (Swiss Cheese Plant)	●										
Myrtus (Myrtle)	●							●			

Natal Plum (Carissa)	
Nephrolepsis exalta (Boston Fern)	
Nerium (Oleander)	
Nightshade (Solanum)	
Octopus Tree (Schefflera)	
Oleander (Nerium)	
Orange Tree, Dwarf (Citrus)	
Oxalis (Oxalis)	
Painted Nettle (Coleus)	
Palms (Caryota,	Suckers.
Chamaedorea,	Suckers.
Chamaerops,	Suckers.
Howeia,	Suckers.
Neanthe,	Suckers.
Palmaceae,	Suckers.
Phoenix)	Suckers.
Pandanus (Screw Pine)	Suckers.
Pandaplant (Kalanchoe tomentosa)	

The Plants	Softwood cuttings	Hardwood cuttings	Root cuttings	Division	Layering	Grafting	Budding	Offsets	Seed	Stratification	Comments
Passiflora (Passion Flower)	●								●		
Patience Plant (Impatiens)	●								●		
Peacock Plant (Episcia)	●										
Pelargonium (Geranium)	●										
Pellaea (Cliff Brake)			●						●		Spores.
Pellionia (Pellionia)	●										
Peperomia (Peperomia)	●										Leaf cuttings work too.
Periwinkle (Vinca)	●		●	●					●		
Persea americana (Avocado)	●								●		
Philodendron (Philodendron)	●			●					●		
Piggyback Plant (Tolmiea)	●										
Pilea cadierei (Aluminum Plant)	●										
Pilea microphyla (Artillery Plant)	●										
Pittosporum tobira (Pittosporum)	●										
Platycerium (Staghorn Ferns)			●						●		Spores.
Plectranthus coleoides (Swedish Ivy)	●								●		
Podocarpus (Yew)	●										
Poinsettia (Euphorbia pulcherrima)	●										

Polypodium (Resurrection Fern, Polypody)	Spores.
Polyscias (Polyscias)	
Pomegranate (Punica granatum)	Dormant cuttings.
Pothos (Scindapsus)	
Prayer Plant (Maranta leuconeura)	
Prickly Pear (Opuntia microdasys)	
Primula (Primrose)	
Pteris (Brake Fern)	Spores.
Punica granatum (Pomegranate)	Dormant cuttings.
Rat Tail Cactus (Aporocactus)	
Resurrection Fern (Polypodium)	
Rhoicissus (Evergreen Treebine)	
Rosary Plant (Ceropegia)	
Rubber Plant (Ficus elastica)	
Saintpaulia (African Violet)	Divide multi-crowned plants.
Sagittaria (Arrowhead Plant)	
Sansevieria (Snake Plant)	
Saxifraga (Strawberry Geranium)	

The Plants

	Softwood cuttings	Hardwood cuttings	Root cuttings	Division	Layering	Grafting	Budding	Offsets	Seed	Stratification	Comments
Schefflera (Octopus Tree)				●							
Scindapsus (Pothos, Ivy-arum)	●			●							
Sea Grape (Coccoloba)								●			
Sedge (Carex)			●								
Sedum (Stonecrop)	●		●					●			
Sempervivum (Houseleek)			●					●			
Senecio cruentus (Cineraria)	●	●	●					●			
Setaria (Foxtail)			●					●			
Shrimp Plant (Beloperone)	●		●								
Sinningia (Gloxinia)	●							●			
Snake Plant (Sansevieria)	●	●	●								
Solanum (Nightshade, Jerusalem Cherry)	●							●			
Spider Plant (Chlorophytum elatum)	●			●							
Spleenwort (Asplenium)			●								
Split Leaf Philodendron (Monstera deliciosa)	●										
Stag's Horn Fern (Platycerium)			●					●			
Star Cactus (Astrophytum)	●										
Stonecrop (Sedum)	●		●					●			

Strelitzia reginae (Bird of Paradise)			
Streptocarpus (Cape Primrose)			
Strawberry Geranium (Saxifraga sarmentosa)			
Swedish Ivy (Plectranthus Coleoides)			
Sweet Flag, Japanese (Acorus)			
Swiss Cheese Plant (Monstera deliciosa)			
Thunbergia (Thunbergia, Clockvine)			
Ti Plant (Cordyline terminalis)			
Tolmiea (Piggyback Plant)			
Tradescantia (Wandering Jew)			
Treebine (Cissus)			
Treebine, Evergreen (Rhoicissus)			
Umbrella Plant (Cyperus alternifolius)			
Umbrella Tree (Brassaia)			
Velvetplant (Gynura)			
Vinca (Periwinkle)			

The Plants

	Softwood cuttings	Hardwood cuttings	Root cuttings	Division	Layering	Grafting	Budding	Offsets	Seed	Stratification	Comments
Wandering Jew (Zebrina)	●										
Wandering Jew (Tradescantia)	●										
Waxplant (Hoya)	●										
Zantedeschia (Calla)								●			
Zebrina (Wandering Jew)	●										

Trees, Shrubs and Assorted Outdoor Plants

The Plants	Softwood cuttings	Hardwood cuttings	Root cuttings	Division	Layering	Grafting	Budding	Offsets	Seed	Stratification	Comments
Abelia (Abelia)	●	●						●			
Abeliophyllum Distinchum (White Forsythia)	●	●						●			
Abies (Fir)					●			●	●		Stratify seeds for 3 months at about 40°.
Acanthopanaz (Aralia)	●	●									
Acer (Maple)				●	●	●	●	●	●		Stratify seeds for 4 months at about 40°.
Achillea (Yarrow)	●			●							
Aconitum (Monkshood)				●				●			
Aesculus (Chestnut)					●			●	●		Stratify seeds for 3 months at about 40°.
African Lily (Agapanthus)			●	●							
Agapanthus (African Lily)			●	●							
Ailanthus (Heaven Tree)			●			●		●	●		Stratify seeds for 2 months at about 40°.
Ajuga (Bugle)				●				●			
Albizia (Silk Tree)		●									
Alder (Alnus)					●			●	●		Some varieties need seed stratification.

The Plants

The Plants	Softwood cuttings	Hardwood cuttings	Root cuttings	Division	Layering	Grafting	Budding	Offsets	Seed	Stratification	Comments
Almond (*Prunus*)	●					●	●	●	●	●	Stratify seeds for 4 months at about 40°.
Alnus (Alder)					●			●	●	●	Some varieties need seed stratification.
Alyssum (Basket of Gold)	●		●					●			
Andromeda (*Pieris*)	●	●						●			
Anemone, bulbous (Anemone)		●	●					●			
Angelica Tree (*Aralia elata*)		●	●					●	●	●	Stratify seeds 5 months warm, then 3 months at 40°.
Apple (*Malus*)					●	●		●			
Aquilegia (Columbine)								●			
Aralia (*Acanthopanax*)	●		●								
Aralia elata (Angelica Tree)		●	●					●	●	●	Stratify seeds 5 months warm, then 3–4 months at 40°.
Araucaria (Araucaria)	●								●		
Arborvitae (*Thuja*)	●	●							●	●	Stratify seeds 2 months at about 40°.
Arbutus unedo (Strawberry Tree)	●				●						
Arenaria (Sandwort)	●			●				●			
Aronia (Chokeberry)	●	●		●	●	●	●	●	●	●	Stratify seeds 3 months at about 40°.
Ash (*Fraxinus*)						●	●	●	●	●	Stratification requirements vary.
Astilbe (Astilbe)				●				●			
Aucuba (Aucuba)	●										

Azalea (Rhododendron)	
Bald Cypress (Taxodium)	Stratify seeds 3 months at about 40°.
Bamboo	
Barberry (Berberis)	Stratify seeds 2 months at about 40°.
Bay Berry (Myrica)	Stratify seeds 2 months at about 40°.
Bay Laurel (Lauris nobilis)	
Basket of Gold (Alyssum)	
Beauty Berry (Callicarpa)	
Beech (Fagus)	Stratify seeds for 3 months at about 40°.
Begonia	
Begonia, tuberous	
Bellflower (Campanula)	
Berberis (Barberry)	Stratify seeds for 2-3 months at about 40°.
Betulla (Birch)	Sow when seeds are ripe or store dry.
Birch (Betulla)	Sow when seeds are ripe or store dry.
Blanket Flower (Gaillarda)	
Bluebeard (Caryopteris)	
Boxwood (Buxus)	
Broom (Cytisus)	Soak seeds overnight before planting.

The Plants

Plant	Softwood cuttings	Hardwood cuttings	Root cuttings	Division	Layering	Grafting	Budding	Offsets	Seed	Stratification	Comments
Bugle (Ajuga)				●							
Buckthorn (Rhamnus)	●	●			●				●	●	Stratify seeds 4 months at about 40°.
Bush Clover (Lespedeza)	●							●			
Buxus (Boxwood)	●	●						●			
Callicarpa (Beauty Berry)	●	●						●			
Calluna (Heather)	●	●		●							
Calycanthus (Sweet Shrub)	●			●					●	●	Stratify seeds 3 months at about 40°.
Campanula (Bellflower)			●	●							
Campsis (Trumpet Vine)	●	●			●			●	●	●	Stratify seeds for 2 months at about 40°.
Caragana (Pea Tree)	●	●				●		●	●	●	Soak seeds overnight before planting.
Carpinus (Hornbeam)					●	●		●	●	●	Stratify seeds 3 months at about 40°.
Caryopteris (Bluebeard)	●			●				●			
Castanea (Spanish Chestnut)					●	●		●	●	●	Stratify seeds for 3 months at about 40°.
Catalpa (Catalpa)	●	●						●			
Catananche (Cupid's Dart)								●			
Ceanothus (Ceanothus)	●	●						●	●	●	Soak overnight, then stratify seeds 3 months at 40°.
Cedrus (Cedar)					●			●	●	●	Stratify seeds for 2 months at about 40°.

Celtis (Hackberry)	Stratify seeds for 3 months at about 40°.
Cephalotaxus (Plum Yew)	Stratify seeds for 3 months at about 40°.
Cercis (Judas Tree)	Soak overnight, then stratify seeds for 2 months at about 40°.
Chestnut (Aesculus)	Stratify seeds for 3 months at about 40°.
Chaenomeles (Quince)	Stratify seeds for 2 months at about 40°.
Chamaecyparis (False Cypress)	Stratify seeds for 3 months at about 40°.
Cherry (Prunus)	Stratify seeds for 4 months at about 40°.
Chimonanthus (Wintersweet)	
Chokeberry (Aronia)	Stratify seeds 3-4 months at about 40°.
Chrysanthemum (Chrysanthemum)	
Cinquefoil (Potentilla)	
Clematis (Clematis)	Stratify seeds for 3 months at about 40°.
Clethra (Clethra)	
Clivia (Kaffir Lily)	
Columbine (Aquilegia)	
Coral Bells (Heuchera)	
Cornus (Dogwood)	Stratify seeds for 3 months at about 40°.
Corylopsis (Winter Hazel)	Double dormant seeds, requirements vary.
Corylus (Hazel Nut)	Stratify seeds for 3 months at about 40°.

The Plants	Softwood cuttings	Hardwood cuttings	Root cuttings	Division	Layering	Grafting	Budding	Offsets	Seed	Stratification	Comments
Cotinus (Smoke Tree)	●				●				●	●	Double dormant seeds, requirements vary.
Cotoneaster (Cotoneaster)	●				●			●	●	●	Soak overnight, then stratify seeds 3 months at about 40°.
Cowslip (Primula)			●					●			
Crane's Bill (*Geranium*)	●		●					●			
Crab Apple (*Malus*)					●	●		●	●	●	Stratify seeds for 3 months at about 40°.
Crape Myrtle (*Lagerstroemia indica*)	●							●			
Crataegus (Hawthorn)		●						●	●	●	Double dormant seeds, requirements vary.
Crocus (Crocus)			●					●			Divide in the early fall.
Cryptomeria (Cryptomeria)	●	●						●			
Cupressus (Cupressus)	●				●			●			
Currant, flowering (*Ribes*)	●	●		●							
Cytisus (Broom)	●	●						●	●		Abrade and soak seeds before planting.
Daboecia (Irish Heath)	●	●	●					●			
Daffodils (*Narcissus*)			●				●	●			
Dahlia (Dahlia)	●		●								Divide so that each piece 'sees'.
Daphne (Daphne)	●	●	●								

Davidia (Dove Tree, Ghost Tree)	Stratify seeds warm for 5 months, then 3 months at about 40°.
Day Lily (*Hemerocallis*)	
Delphinium (Delphinium)	
Deutzia (Deutzia)	
Dianthus (Pinks)	
Diervilla (Bush Honeysuckle)	
Digitalis (Foxglove)	
Diospyros (Persimmon)	Stratify seeds for 3 months at about 40°.
Dogwood (*Cornus*)	Stratify seeds for 3 months at about 40°.
Dove Tree (*Davidia*)	Stratify seeds warm for 5 months, then 3 months at about 40°.
Edelweiss (*Leontopodium*)	
Elaeagnus (Oleaster)	Stratify seeds warm for 4-5 months, then 3 months at about 40°.
Elderberry (*Sambucus*)	Stratify seeds for 3 months at about 40°.
Elm (*Ulmus*)	
Erica (Heath)	
Eucalyptus (Eucalyptus)	

The Plants	Softwood cuttings	Hardwood cuttings	Root cuttings	Division	Layering	Grafting	Budding	Offsets	Seed	Stratification	Comments
Euonymous (Euonymous)	●	●									
Exochorda (Pearl Bush)	●	●	●					●			
Fagus (Beech)					●				●		Stratify seeds for 3 months at about 40°.
False Cypress (*Chamaecyparis*)		●			●	●		●	●		Stratify seeds for 4 months at about 40°.
Ferns			●					●			Spores.
Ficus (Fig)		●	●	●							
Fir (*Abies*)	●					●		●	●		Stratify seeds for 4 months at about 40°.
Firethorn (*Pyracantha*)	●				●	●		●	●		Stratify seeds for 3 months at about 40°.
Flax (*Linum*)	●		●					●			
Forsythia (Forsythia)	●	●	●	●							
Forsythia, white (*Abeliophyllum distichum*)	●	●						●			
Fothergilla (Fothergilla)	●				●			●	●		Stratify seeds for 4 months warm, then 3 months at about 40°.
Foxglove (*Digitalis*)				●							
Frangipani (*Plumeria*)	●										
Fraxinus (Ash)						●	●	●	●		Stratification requirements vary.
Fuchsia (Fuchsia)	●							●			

Plant	Col 1	Col 2	Col 3	Col 4	Col 5	Col 6	Notes
Gaillarda (Blanket Flower)	●			●			
Geranium (Crane's Bill)	●			●		●	
Geranium (*Pelargonium*)	●		●	●			
Ginkgo (Ginkgo)	●					●	
Gladiolus (Gladiolus)	●			●			Corms.
Gloxinia (*Sinningia speciosa*)	●					●	
Gum, sweet (*Liquidamar*)	●	●					Stratify seeds for 3 months at about 40°.
Halesia (Silver Bell)	●	●					Stratify seeds warm for 4 months, then 3 months at about 40°.
Hamamelis (Witch Hazel)	●	●	●			●	Double dormant seeds, requirements vary.
Hawthorn (*Crataegus*)	●	●	●		●		Double dormant seeds, requirements vary.
Hazel Nut (*Corylus*)	●	●		●		●	Stratify seeds for 3 months at about 40°.
Heath (*Erica*)	●	●		●		●	
Heather (*Calluna*)	●			●		●	
Hedera (Ivy)	●			●		●	
Hemerocallis (Day Lily)	●				●		
Hemlock (*Tsuga*)	●	●	●	●		●	Stratify seeds for 3 months at about 40°.
Heuchera (Coral Bells)	●	●			●		

	Softwood cuttings	Hardwood cuttings	Root cuttings	Division	Layering	Grafting	Budding	Offsets	Seed	Stratification	Comments
Hibiscus (Hibiscus)	●										
Hippophae (Sea Buckthorn)		●	●	●							
Holly (Ilex)	●	●						●			Seeds are reported to be disappointing.
Honeysuckle (Lonicera)	●	●	●	●				●	●		Stratify seeds for 3 months at about 40°.
Hornbeam (Carpinus)						●		●	●	●	Stratify seeds for 3 months at about 40°.
Houseleek (Sempervivum)			●					●			
Hydrangea (Hydrangea)	●							●			
Hypericum (St. John's Wort)	●	●	●					●			
Ilex (Holly)	●	●									Absolutely no luck reported with seeds.
Iris (Iris)			●	●							
Irish Heath (Daboecia)	●	●						●			
Ivy (Hedera)	●	●						●			
Jasminum (Jasmine)	●			●				●			
Judas Tree (Cercis siliquastrum)	●				●			●	●	●	Soak seeds overnight, then stratify for 2 months at about 40°.
Juglans (Black Walnut)								●	●	●	Stratify seeds for 4 months at about 40°.

Juniperus (Juniper)	Stratify seeds warm for 3 months, then 3 months at about 40°.
Kaffir Lily (*Clivia*)	
Kalmia (Mountain Laurel)	
Kerria (Kerria)	
Laburnum (Laburnum)	Soak seeds overnight before planting.
Lagerstroemia indica (Crape Myrtle)	
Lantana (Lantana)	
Larix (Larch)	Stratify seeds for 3 months at about 40°.
Lauris nobilis (Bay Laurel)	
Lavandula (Lavender)	
Leontopodium (Edelweiss)	
Lespedeza (Bush Clover)	
Ligustrum (Privet)	Stratify seeds for 3 months at about 40°.
Lilac (*Syringa*)	
Lily (*Lilium*)	Cuttings are taken with bulbils attached.
Linum (Flax)	
Liquidamar (Sweet Gum)	Stratify seeds for 3 months at about 40°.
Lobelia (Lobelia)	

The Plants

	Softwood cuttings	Hardwood cuttings	Root cuttings	Division	Layering	Grafting	Budding	Offsets	Seed	Stratification	Comments
Locust (*Robinia*)			•						•		Soak seeds overnight before planting.
Lonicera (Honeysuckle)	•	•		•					•	•	Stratify seeds for 3 months at about 40°.
Magnolia (Magnolia)	•								•	•	Stratify seeds for 3–4 months at about 40°.
Mahonia (Mahonia)	•		•						•	•	Stratify seeds for 3 months at about 40°.
Malus (Apple, Crab Apple)						•	•		•	•	Stratify seeds for 3 months at about 40°.
Maple (*Acer*)				•	•	•			•	•	Stratify seeds for 4 months at about 40°.
Metasequoia (Redwood)	•	•							•		
Mock Orange (*Philadelphus*)	•	•		•					•		
Monkshood (*Aconitum*)				•					•		
Morus (Mulberry)	•	•							•	•	Stratify seeds for 3 months at about 40°.
Mountain Laurel (*Kalmia*)	•	•							•		
Mulberry (*Morus*)	•	•	•						•	•	Stratify seeds for 3 months at about 40°.
Myrica (Bayberry)	•								•	•	Soak seeds, then stratify for 2 months at about 40°.
Narcissus (Daffodils)								•			
Nerium (Oleander)	•										

Oleander (*Nerium*)	
Oleaster (*Elaeagnus*)	Stratify seeds warm for 4 months, then 3 months at about 40°.
Osmanthus (Osmanthus)	Berries.
Oxydendrum (Sorel)	
Paeonia (Peony, herbaceous)	
Paeonia (Tree Peony)	Stratify seeds warm for 4-5 months, then 3 months at about 40°.
Pagoda Tree (*Sophora*)	Soak seeds overnight before planting.
Parthenocissus (Virginia Creeper)	
Passiflora (Passion Flower)	
Pea Tree (*Caragana*)	
Pear (*Pyrus*)	Stratify seeds for 3 months at about 40°.
Pearl Bush (*Exochorda*)	
Pelargonium (Geranium)	
Periwinkle (*Vinca*)	
Persimmon (*Diospyrus*)	Stratify seeds for 3 months at about 40°.
Philadelphus (Mock Orange)	
Phlox (Phlox)	

The Plants

	Softwood cuttings	Hardwood cuttings	Root cuttings	Division	Layering	Grafting	Budding	Offsets	Seed	Stratification	Comments
Picea (Spruce)	●	●				●			●	●	Stratify seeds for 4 months at about 40°.
Pieris (Andromeda)	●	●						●			
Pinks (*Dianthus*)	●		●	●							
Pinus (Pine)	●					●			●	●	Stratify seeds for 4 months at about 40°.
Plum (*Prunus*)	●					●	●		●	●	Stratify seeds for 4 months at about 40°.
Plumbago (Plumbago)	●							●			
Plumeria (Frangipani)	●										
Pomegranate (*Punica*)	●							●			
Populus (Poplar)	●	●			●						
Potentilla (Shrub Cinquefoil)	●	●	●					●			
Primula (Primrose, Cowslip)			●					●			
Privet (*Ligustrum*)	●	●							●	●	Stratify seeds for 3 months at about 40°.
Prunus (Cherry, Almond, Plum)	●					●	●		●	●	Stratify seeds for 4 months at about 40°.
Pterocarya (Wingnut)				●		●		●	●	●	Stratify seeds for 4 months at about 40°.
Punica (Pomegranate)	●							●			
Pyracantha (Firethorn)	●	●				●		●	●	●	Stratify seeds for 3 months at about 40°.
Pyrus (Pear)						●	●	●	●	●	Stratify seeds for 3 months at about 40°.

Comments

Plant	Remarks
Quercus (Oak)	Stratify seeds for 4 months at about 40°.
Quince (*Chaenomeles*)	Stratify seeds for 2 months at about 40°.
Redwood (*Metasequoia*)	
Rhamnus (Buckthorn)	Stratify seeds for 4 months at about 40°.
Rhododendron (Rhododendron)	
Rhododendron (Azalea)	
Rhus (Sumac)	Stratify seeds warm for 4-5 months, then 4 months at about 40°.
Ribes (Flowering Currant)	Stratify seeds for 3 months at about 40°.
Robinia (Acacia, Locust)	Soak seeds overnight before planting.
Rosa (Rose)	Stratify seeds for 3 months at about 40°.
Salix (Willow)	
Sambucus (Elderberry)	Stratify seeds for 3 months at about 40°.
Sassafras (Sassafras)	Stratify seeds for 3-4 months at about 40°.
Sciadopitys (Umbrella Pine)	
Sea Buckthorn (*Hippophae*)	
Sedum (Stonecrop)	
Sempervivum (Houseleek)	

The Plants	Softwood cuttings	Hardwood cuttings	Root cuttings	Division	Layering	Grafting	Budding	Offsets	Seed	Stratification	Comments
Sequoia (Redwood)	•								•	•	Stratify seeds for 3 months at about 40°.
Silk Tree (*Albizia*)		•						•			
Silver Bell (*Halesia*)								•	•	•	Stratify seeds for 4 months warm, then for 3 months at about 40°.
Sinningia speciosa (Gloxinia)	•							•			
Skimmia (Skimmia)	•	•						•			
Smoke Tree (*Cotinus*)	•			•				•	•	•	Double dormant seeds, requirements vary.
Sophora (Pagoda Tree)	•							•	•		Soak seeds overnight before planting.
Sorbaria (False Spirea)	•	•	•					•	•		
Sorbus (Mountain Ash)					•			•	•	•	Stratify seeds for 3 months at about 40°.
Sorel (*Oxydendrum*)	•							•	•		
Spanish Chestnut (*Castanea*)					•	•		•	•	•	Stratify seeds for 3 months at about 40°.
Spirea (Spirea)	•	•						•	•		
Spruce (*Picea*)	•	•				•		•	•	•	Stratify seeds for 4 months at about 40°.
St. John's Wort (*Hypericum*)	•	•	•					•	•		
Stewartia (Stewartia)	•			•				•	•	•	Stratify seeds for 3-4 months at about 40°.
Stonecrop (*Sedum*)	•		•					•			
Strawberry Tree (*Arbutus unedo*)	•										

Plant	Remarks
Sumac (*Rhus*)	Stratify seeds warm for 5 months, then 4 months at about 40°.
Sweet Shrub (*Calycanthus floridus*)	Stratify seeds for 3 months at about 40°.
Symphoricarpos (Snowberries)	
Syringa (Lilac)	
Tamarix (Tamarisk)	
Taxodium (Bald Cypress)	Stratify seeds for 3 months at about 40°.
Taxus (Yew)	Stratify seeds for 5 months warm, then 4 months at about 40°.
Thuja (Arborvitae)	Stratify seeds for 3 months at about 40°.
Trumpet Vine (*Campsis*)	Stratify seeds for 2 months at about 40°.
Tsuga (Hemlock)	Stratify seeds for 3 months at about 40°.
Ulmus (Elm)	
Umbrella Pine (*Sciadopitys*)	
Viburnum (Viburnum)	Stratify seeds for 4 months warm, then 3 months at about 40°.
Vinca (Periwinkle)	

The Plants	Softwood cuttings	Hardwood cuttings	Root cuttings	Division	Layering	Grafting	Budding	Offsets	Seed	Stratification	Comments
Viola (Violet)				•					•		
Virginia Creeper (Parthenocissus)	•	•		•					•		
Vitis (Vitis)	•	•		•					•	•	Stratify seeds for 3 months at about 40°.
Walnut, Black (Juglans)									•	•	Stratify seeds for 4 months at about 40°.
Weigela (Weigela)	•	•						•			
Willow (Salix)	•	•	•					•	•		
Windflower (Anemonella)		•	•					•	•		
Wingnut (Pterocarya)	•		•	•				•	•	•	Stratify seeds for 4 months at about 40°.
Winter Hazel (Corylopsis)	•				•			•	•	•	Double dormant seeds, requirements vary.
Wintersweet (Chimonanthus)				•				•	•		
Wisteria (Wisteria)	•	•		•	•			•	•	•	Soak seeds overnight before planting.
Witch Hazel (Hamamelis)	•			•	•			•	•	•	Double dormant seeds, requirements vary.
Yarrow (Achillea)	•		•								
Yew (Taxus)								•	•	•	Stratify seeds for 5 months warm, then 4 months at about 40°.
Yucca (Yucca)		•	•								Divide side shoots.